mood food

brighten, heal and elevate your state of mind

mood food

brighten, heal and elevate your state of mind

by Jane Eldershaw

SOURCEBOOKS, INC.®
NAPERVILLE, ILLINOIS

This publication is designed to provide accurate and authoritative information in regard to the subject matter covered. It is sold with the understanding that the publisher is not engaged in rendering legal, accounting, or other professional services. If legal advice or other expert assistance is required, the services of a competent professional person should be sought.—*From a Declaration of Principles Jointly Adopted by a Committee of the American Bar Association and a Committee of Publishers and Associations*

This book is not intended as a medical guide or manual for self-treatment. If you have psychological or medical problems, please seek competent medical care. Nutritional needs vary greatly from person to person. You must consult a health-care professional before taking supplements or changing your diet.

Published by Sourcebooks, Inc.
P.O. Box 4410, Naperville, Illinois 60567-4410
(630) 961-3900
FAX: (630) 961-2168

Library of Congress Cataloging-in-Publication Data

Eldershaw, Jane.
  Mood food: brighten, heal and elevate your state of mind / by Jane Eldershaw.
    p. cm.
  ISBN 1-57071-713-3 (alk. paper)
    1. Mental health—Nutritional aspects. 2. Health—Nutritional aspects. 3. Mood (Psychology) 4. Cookery. I. Title

  RC455.4.N8 E43 2001
  613.2—dc21

                                                          00-066155

Printed and bound in the United States of America
BG 10 9 8 7 6 5 4 3 2 1

Acknowledgments

With love and gratitude to Sheree Bykofsky, Alison Clark, Dee Anne Dyke, Susan Hurley, Cynthia Kilian, George Ladas, Deborah Werksman, and especially Elisabeth MacIntyre.

Table of Contents

Foreword

Anyone who's ever baked bread knows what good therapy this can be. Rhythmically kneading the dough, smartly punching it down after it has risen, and shaping the springy mass into smooth loaves is every bit as rewarding as biting into the finished product, hot and fragrant from the oven.

In today's microwave-paced world, we're apt to forget that the "comfort" in comfort food can come as much from cooking the things that make us feel nurtured as from eating them. In her book, *Mood Food*, Jane Eldershaw explains not only the dietary reasons why certain foods might brighten a bad day, but also how the creative process of preparing them can have its own positive effect.

And, if you think comfort food invariably means fattening food, you'll be glad to see that these recipes are made with low-fat ingredients. Gaining unwanted pounds, after all, is on no one's list of mood enhancers.

On and off over the years, Jane and I worked together under the pressure of meeting newspaper deadlines. On these pages, she shares her stress-busting secrets, as well as culinary cures for other forms of malaise.

They could be the best thing since sliced bread for lifting your spirits.

Cynthia Kilian,
New York Post Food Critic

Introduction

For years, my father persisted in wearing my very first knitting project, a long, multicolored scarf. It was lumpy with knots, holey with dropped stitches, and skinny and wide by turns as it snaked through thin and fat patches of different weights of wool.

As I grew older, I became more and more annoyed that he continued to wind this scrawny thing around his neck. People would comment on it—I hated the amusement in their voices—and Dad would proudly point out deficiencies they may otherwise have missed: gaps, loose strands, and patches of back-to-front pattern.

For me, the thing was living evidence of my failures and mistakes, inadequacies and incompetence. But to him, it was a work of art—a testament to the pain and triumphs and struggles of learning. It had the shape of personal experience.

Life is like that scarf. Good patches and bad patches. Homemade. A learning experience. The successes right there with the failures, misadventures, and calamities.

It misses the point to label it "good" or "bad"—it just is what it is. But when you're upset, it's hard to be that objective about life.

> "How good one feels when one is full—how satisfied with ourselves and with the world! People who have tried it, tell me that a clear conscience makes you very happy and contented; but a full stomach does the business quite as well, and is cheaper, and more easily obtained."
>
> —From *Three Men in a Boat* by Jerome K. Jerome, 1889

That's when you need good friends for a healthy dose of reality and laughter over a glass of wine and a home-cooked meal. They usually have sensible words of advice, but more than that, there's great comfort in the affinity of fellowship, in the realization that we all have similar problems, and in the knowledge that others have been there and suffered the same way we suffer.

Both physically and psychologically, food is an especially important part of the nurturing process. Life goes on; our bodies and minds constantly renew themselves, and we need fuel for the journey. Sharing a cup of coffee and a cookie with a caring friend feeds your body and feeds your soul.

I'd like to think that this book provides the same sort of healing and nurturing. When your life becomes tangled and knotted, I hope you'll find this book something to turn to for comforting food to eat and for helpful insights to think about.

How We Think Our Way Into Moods

Of all the insights I've come across, the one that struck me with the force of planets colliding is this: the way I feel is determined by the thoughts I think.

For years, I blamed the whole outside world—traffic lights, timetables, taxes—for making me feel angry, upset, overwrought. I felt that everything and everyone was in collusion to provoke me.

It was hard to accept that I'd chosen to feel these feelings.

Thoughts are the talk radio that's always playing in your head. Feelings are the background music that's picking up the same tone as the voice: passion, frustration, humility, fear, wonder, annoyance, lust, boredom, serenity—the whole range of human emotions. Feelings are changing constantly, going from high to low throughout the day. A feeling is not right or wrong, it's an emotional reaction to a thought. Moods are when thoughts and feelings get stuck in one emotion.

But it all starts with thoughts—thoughts constantly interpreting the events that happen to us.

Nobody teaches kids the right way to talk to themselves. Instead, they're given all sorts of mixed messages in an attempt to make them feel better—or keep them quiet.

For example, perhaps you cried as a toddler when Mom left you in someone else's care. If the babysitter tried to distract you instead of letting you acknowledge and cope with the pain of abandonment, she gave you one of your first lessons in not dealing with your feelings directly.

Or maybe, as a child, you told your mother you hated your sister, and she reacted with shock and horror, insisting, "No, no, no—you love your sister!" You learned not to trust your own emotions.

Dealing with your emotions would seem to be a simple thing to learn, something an objective, grown-up individual ought to be able to absorb and remember. But life is not tidy, some problems don't have solutions, and a full, rich life comes with patches of melancholy, lethargy, and general malaise, even when you know how to manage moods. Nothing automatically makes human beings perpetually happy. Life is great one day, lousy the next. We spend our lives seeking happiness and avoiding pain, ricocheting between the two because neither the happiness nor the pain lasts. So we keep learning life lessons over and over.

I had originally planned to write a book that outlined basic moods and healthy ways of dealing with them in bite-sized morsels of adult perspective. I envisioned wisdom in a simple format, the instant or powdered variety. I thought feeling good was all about correcting your thinking.

Then I found out I had osteoporosis.

Brain Food

I couldn't believe I hadn't been getting enough calcium in my diet. I thought I ate pretty well: skim milk in my morning coffee; lots of cheese, yogurt, and sour cream. I stay away from most junk food, take a multivitamin daily. Where did I go wrong?

To find out, I started reading about psychonutrition.

I discovered that by not getting enough calcium, I'd been missing out not only on strong bones and teeth, but on a substance that reduces mood swings, irritability, depression, and mental confusion. Calcium not only does all that, but, in the process it also boosts alertness and good mood. Who knew?

And how can a food do all that?

It seems that although the brain accounts for only 2 percent of body weight, it uses about one-quarter of all the calories you eat.

The brain needs food to make essential neurotransmitters. You drop something. Your neurons, the smallest nerve cells, communicate the news through the nervous system to the brain. The message jumps from neuron to neuron, across a gap called a synapse, with the help of neurotransmitters. The thought "Oops!" surfaces, and more messages are passed through the nervous system to your hands, which fumble for the object. It's a practically instantaneous relay, happening all day long, with every thought and impulse.

Nutrients from food pass from your blood to your brain and combine with brain enzymes to make amino acids or choline— which are what neurotransmitters are made up of. Too little of the right sort of nutrients and the body stops production of neuro-transmitters, causing you to experience changes in mood, appetite, and thinking. Your motor skills slow down. Vitamins help neuro-transmitter activity and protect them from damage.

The neurotransmitter most strongly influenced by your diet is serotonin. High levels boost your mood, curb food cravings, increase pain tolerance, and help you sleep. Low levels may cause insomnia, aggressive behavior, poor body temperature regulation, and depression.

Then there are endorphins, chemicals your body makes that pro-duce a feeling of well-being to help you tolerate pain and stress. Laughter, meditation, and soothing music raise endorphin levels—as well as sweet foods. Eating them releases endorphins, which make you feel so good they leave you craving more.

We've also evolved to crave fat—long-term storage fuel for the body. You are calmed by eating creamy, gooey, flavorful foods high in fat which enhance the action of galanin, a brain chemical that makes you feel better. That's why so many high-fat items are called comfort foods.

The bad guys are free radicals, the prime suspect for every ill the body is heir to, from cancer to Alzheimers. What you eat can neu-tralize their effects, too.

Food not only benefits us nutritionally, giving the body nutri-ents it needs to thrive, but physically, by providing elements like fiber, and pharmacologically, by providing protective substances.

But, OK, that's enough science.

The reading I've done has convinced me it's very complicated. Every day, each of us is balanced, it seems, by slight changes in blood sugar levels, placing us on a biological tightrope between coma and convulsions. And everyone is biochemically unique, with different abilities to synthesize the chemicals in food.

Basically, carbohydrates are comfort foods that make you feel less stressed, while proteins tend to make you more alert, but, of course, it's not that simple. All the amino acids that get into the blood stream fight with each other to enter the brain. The combination of food you eat at a meal determines which ones make it.

To structure the optimal diet for yourself, you'd need to be an orthomolecular psychiatrist. But the take-home lesson is: what you eat has a very real effect on your mood.

Eating Healthy

I always knew I should eat healthy foods, but when I was young, the consequences of doing so seemed a long way off. Also, I had an idea that my body would tell me what it needed, that if I had a deficiency in iron, for example, I'd get a craving for meat. But it doesn't always work that way. Have you ever wondered why it's all things unwise and wonderful that make you feel good when, if nutritionists and the U.S. Department of Agriculture's Food Guide Pyramid are right, it should be fresh fruit and vegetables that make you feel whole, healthy, and happy?

Back in hunter-gatherer days, sweet foods and fat were few and far between, but necessary for survival. Our preference for sweets developed because bitter roots and plants often are poisonous. You feel good after eating something sweet because of the initial endorphin boost, followed by a lingering good mood as serotonin slowly increases. You want to eat more. Our bodies evolved to love fat and sweets as a survival mechanism. Today, when there are far too many of them around, you have to take responsibility for what you eat.

These are the guidelines, and you've heard it all before: maintain a healthy weight, stay hydrated, get five to nine servings a day of fruit and vegetables (including one citrus fruit and one food rich in antioxidants such as spinach or tomatoes). Choose whole grains, beans, yogurt, and fewer processed foods. Take a daily multivitamin. Eat breakfast. Try to consume twenty to twenty-five different foods daily.

Sounds like a full-time job.

Is it worth it? Will eating a healthy diet improve the quality of your life? Well, what it will do is give you energy, keep you at a healthy weight, and cut down your risk of cancer and heart disease. The main benefits of a healthy-as-you-can-make-it, reduced-fat diet are a decrease in the occurrence of post-indulgence regret after a large meal, an increase in the number of helpings you can allow yourself to consume, and the smug, self-satisfied feeling of the insufferably virtuous.

However, there is no guarantee that even a healthy diet will keep you happy all the time. The trouble with psychonutrition is that there are so many variables. And, of course, you can never expect all your problems to disappear.

But the truth is, food does affect mood, and we're all familiar with the way food can be used to comfort ourselves, to connect with another person, or to soothe the five-year-old self who is having a tantrum.

To feel good, you need both to manage your thoughts *and* to manage your food.

Moods

There are three kinds of moods detailed in this book. There are the moods that come from inner conflict, like anger and worry and feeling old. There are moods that inevitably come from interacting—or not—with others: jealousy, guilt, and loneliness. And the moods that come from outer and inner pressures, such as stress, feeling fat, or feeling poor.

I think most women become aware of their changing moods when they become aware of the shifting hormones in their bodies every month. We live within a cycle of body and mood mixes—the range depends on the individual—and we learn to manage them to a certain extent.

The constructive way to manage a mood is really to feel what you're feeling. Don't resist. Don't try to distract yourself, to deny the emotion, to fight it, or to hide from it.

Feel it deeply, go with the flow. Be in tune with the mood until it passes like a thunderstorm, clearing the air. You'll feel something loosen up inside that you hadn't known was tight.

Feeling lousy actually can be productive because the hurt points out what's important in your life, and what needs to change. To manage painful feelings, you are going to need to identify them, to express them, and to analyze their meaning, while at the same time trying to control their potentially negative effects.

Being in a "bad" mood can be an opportunity to get in touch with yourself and to nurture and take care of yourself.

Food Can Heal Mood

In one of the *Peanuts* cartoons by Charles Schulz, Lucy asks Charlie Brown to make her a sandwich. He makes the sandwich, then picks up a knife. Lucy starts yelling: "Don't cut it! Don't cut it! Just fold it over."

She takes the sandwich, explaining: "When you cut 'em, they lose all their flavor!"

Food is a ritual, a plaything, a psychological comfort.

Food is pure sensual pleasure.

There's the aroma that creates anticipation. Then the artfulness of the presentation—we eat first with our eyes. There's how food feels in the mouth. Crunchy, smooth, chewy—texture is everything. The warmth of food—a steaming hot cup of soup or tea—gives a feeling of comfort and safety the way nothing else can.

Food is a journey back in time, the remembrance of things past.

From our earliest youth, we learn that the four primal survival needs are air, water, love, and ice cream. That the six stages of coping are anger, denial, bargaining, chocolate, acceptance, and hope.

And we all have our favorite comfort food: the solace of soup, the caressing smoothness of custard, the memories in mashed potatoes and meat loaf. Security is served on a spoon.

Food, as all children know, is something to play with. Remember when the pure enjoyment of food unspoiled by calories, time, or manners? Remember squeezing cheese-filled crackers so that the contents squirted out the holes, twisting open Oreos and eating the filling? When the mashed potato was the mountain and the gravy was the lake? Food is a return to the mud pies of childhood.

The adult version of playing with food is cooking. Can you bake your way to a better mood? I say, yes, you can.

Cooking calms. There's the order imposed by the recipe directions, the soul-soothing repetition of dicing and chopping, clearing and measuring, the rhythm of stirring. While you're engrossed in the Zen of preparing food, you're in a state very like meditation, a way of centering yourself. You slow down, your actions become rhythmical, your thinking clear.

While the hands are busy, the mind has space to interpret feelings, think through the causes of unhappiness, mull over problems—a good reason, when you're in a bad mood, to go into the kitchen and play with food (get yourself messy, separate eggs with your fingers, mix meat loaf with your hands) until your soul's cloudy weather clears up.

Food is always at the center of ritual, a way of binding families and communities together. Our grandmothers knew this. When women had no overt power, they had the power of food. For women, food always has been about control, the means of making life sweet, bringing everyone together in picture-perfect moments, presiding over all the good tastes and good times. You feed everyone, they feel better, life is good.

We make a private ritual of food, too. Remember being allowed to choose a chocolate from a box of mixed assortments? The agony that you might get coconut instead of strawberry cream? Sticking a thumb in the bottom when no one was looking to find out which were the caramels?

Sharing food—two straws in one milkshake—is one of the strongest statements we can make about how we feel about someone.

In each section of this book, I've tried to highlight a different use of food. In some sections, I've suggested that it's the actions involved in cooking that help heal the mood—when you're angry, for example, bread dough gives you something to pound at in frustration. At other times, it's the chemical reaction—chocolate really does make you feel better.

Each section of this book has a quick fix to make you feel good fast, a thought to mull over while you're preparing the food, and each recipe comes with a mood-to-food connection. At the end, there's a serving suggestion to provide further actions you might like to take to shift your mood from tempestuous to tranquil.

My goal in writing this book was to provide a place to turn when you're feeling less than wonderful. I hope it will fill you with serenity as well as serotonin.

About the Recipes

The recipes in this book are comfort foods made low-fat.

Most of them can be put together in less time than it takes to reheat a TV dinner or wait for pizza to be delivered or sniff at assorted side dishes from the back of the refrigerator while foraging for leftovers that need to be eaten.

Life is too short to stuff a mushroom. I rely heavily on the blender, the microwave, and fat-free yogurt. Why bother to cook at all, then, you may ask, when there are so many convenience foods available today? For the joy of a muffin hot from the oven—and knowing exactly what's in it. For the relaxation inherent in putting it together. For the joy of serving up a loved one something you've taken the time and made the effort to make from scratch.

I've tried to streamline the recipe instructions as much as possible, but there's one extra step that shouldn't be skipped when making quick breads and muffins, and that's sifting the flour. For years, I never sifted flour when I baked, having decided that recipe writers were overly paranoid about the possibility of there being bugs in my flour. But I finally realized that you aren't sifting to get things out, you're sifting to put air in, and to avoid lumps and to ensure a lighter result. An easy way to sift is to balance a wire sieve (one with two hooks at one end and a handle at the other) over your mixing bowl. Then you can dump the flour (and baking soda and other dry ingredients) right in the sieve as you measure them out. Tap the side of the sieve against the heel of your hand—the flour falls through and you're all done.

The recipes in this book call for canola oil or olive oil, both monounsaturated fats, which are said to lower the bad cholesterol in your blood but not the good.

Egg substitutes are just egg whites plus corn oil, flavorings, and preservatives. If you want to cut down on saturated fat and cholesterol, use two egg whites in place of a whole egg in these recipes. Feed the leftover yolks to the dog, use as a beautifying masque on your face, or make into scrambled eggs or omelets for the kids.

Most of these recipes will feed at least two people—I hesitate to designate amounts because I have known individuals who can devour at one sitting a dessert intended to serve six people—but I've specified where a recipe is enough for just one person.

Remember that the fewer ingredients listed in a recipe, the better quality those ingredients should be. Remember that there's a difference between baking soda and baking powder. Remember to grease all your cake tins with nonfat cooking spray, even the ones with nonstick surfaces—especially the ones with nonstick surfaces.

And most of all, remember that it isn't the destination, it's the journey. Enjoy preparing these easy recipes as much as you enjoy eating their results.

"It is very strange, this domination of our intellect by our digestive organs. We cannot work, we cannot think, unless our stomach wills so. It dictates to us our emotions, our passions. After eggs and bacon, it says 'Work!' After hot muffins, it says 'Be dull and soulless, like a beast of the field.' And after brandy, taken in sufficient quantity, it says, 'Now, come, fool, grin and tumble.'"

—from *Three Men in a Boat* by Jerome K. Jerome, 1889

Angry

If you've ever been surprised by the intensity of your own anger, you know how strong and overwhelming this emotion can be.

It's important to understand where your anger comes from, so you can diffuse it safely. Realize that when you are reacting with anger, you are struggling with yourself. Yes, someone else did something infuriating, but that reminded your subconscious of a deep-down, psychological hurt that it hasn't dealt with yet. You need to let go of the angry reaction—it's hiding something that you have to face up to.

Most little girls are taught to suppress their anger, so women tend to feel that it's counterproductive to act out, but that's not necessarily true.

Anger isn't bad or wrong—it just is. If you express your anger at the time it arises, at the person whose actions made you feel angry, and are able to resolve the issues that aroused the anger, the whole episode actually can be a healing experience.

But if you displace your anger, try to bury it, express it too late, or confuse it with other issues, anger can be destructive. And, not just the

It's frustrating—and useless—to try to force someone who often makes you angry to change their ways. The only person you can control is yourself, the only reactions you can influence are your own.

calm

peaceful

obvious damage you can do by lashing out at a loved one, verbally or physically—you can actually make yourself sick by being constantly in a state of anger.

Sometimes you may not even realize you're angry. You may think of yourself as a good driver, yet be consumed by road rage whenever you're stuck in traffic. (If so, try playing soothing music on the CD player in the car.)

The key to controlling anger is to find different ways of reacting.

Try This First

If you feel out of control, the first step is to get a grip: isolate yourself, go for a walk, simmer down. Even if your anger is entirely justified, you'll be more effective in retaliation if you have control over yourself. Visualize a relaxing, soothing scene, and really focus on it for a few minutes.

Next, ask yourself why you are angry. Diagnose the threat to your well-being. Instead of thinking how you can get back at a person, think how you can change the situation.

Thought to Chew on in the Kitchen

If I wasn't feeling so angry, what other feelings (hurt? fear?) would I be feeling? What's the real reason I'm reacting so strongly to this?

Fury-Fading Focaccia

Therapists say that expressing your anger by pounding a pillow is a bad way to deal with it—physical violence is like pouring fuel on the flames—but repressing your feelings is not good either. The best way of coping is to calm yourself through nonviolent physical activities, then to discuss your problem with the person who triggered your angry response.

So try talking—to someone else or to yourself—and kneading focaccia at the same time. And if you find you're pounding that dough extra hard, that's OK, it'll mean a wonderfully textured bread to break with your opponent when you take it, fragrant, from the oven.

And, bread is a complex carbohydrate, a food which elevates serotonin and tryptophan levels, which in turn alleviates irritability and elevates mood.

Bread takes a while to rise, but then so do some of the world's most creative people, some days. Don't be put off by the long directions, they're mainly easily mastered techniques. If you've made bread before, you know most of this already.

Use your anger to propel you toward constructive action rather than as an excuse for destructive behavior.

forgiveness

Ingredients

1 packet (one-quarter of an ounce) dry yeast

1¼ cups warm water (105° to 112° F, but it's not necessary to get out a thermometer, water from the hot tap is fine)

2 tablespoons of best quality extra virgin olive oil

1 teaspoon salt

3¼ to 3¾ cups all-purpose flour. There's no need to sift flour when you're making bread. If you can find bread flour, which is made from hard winter wheat, use it—you'll need a bit less flour and get a better result. (Don't use cake flour.)

2 heaping tablespoons, or more, dried rosemary

1 medium onion, thinly sliced

1 teaspoon coarse (kosher) salt

more rosemary for decoration

If you think you can put your hands on a clean spray bottle, and like your bread with a crisp crust, go find it now.

Preparation

Keep everything warm. You get the best results when ingredients and utensils are at room temperature and the kitchen has no drafts. Warm the mixing bowl by rinsing it in hot water.

Pour a quarter cup of the hot water into a large mixing bowl. Sprinkle yeast over it, stir briefly, then let stand for five minutes—it should be foaming. Add remaining one cup hot water and one tablespoon oil. Stir in salt and three cups flour. Stir in just enough additional flour to make a soft dough that begins to pull away from the sides of the bowl.

A large wooden board is good to knead on, or use the kitchen countertop if it is completely dry. Sprinkle a little flour on the surface, smooth it with your hand, then place the dough on it. Knead in the rosemary, adding more flour if the dough is sticky, but try not to add much.

Bread dough is not fragile—it needs vigorous handling to develop a smooth, even texture. To knead, pick up the far edge of the dough and fold it over itself toward you. Place your palms on top of it and push down and forward. Push with your whole body, not just with your arms. Turn the dough a quarter turn and repeat the fold-push-turn sequence. Build up a rhythm. Continue to knead for about 8 to 10 minutes until dough is smooth and satiny, and small blisters appear on the surface. To test if the dough has been kneaded enough, make an indentation with your fingers. If the dough springs back, you're done.

Place the dough in a greased bowl and turn to coat all sides. Cover the bowl with plastic wrap or a clean dishcloth. Let dough rise in a warm place (for example, in an unheated oven on the top shelf, with a large pan of hot, steaming water below it) for about 75 minutes, or until doubled in bulk.

Test the dough by poking two fingers about a half inch into the dough. If the holes remain, the dough has risen.

Punch the dough by sinking your fist down to the bottom of the bowl then pulling the dough from the edges into the center hollow. Do this about twenty times.

Preheat the oven to 400° F.

Let the dough rest 10 minutes. Meanwhile, sauté the onion in the remaining tablespoon of oil in a medium skillet until soft. Transfer dough to a lightly greased cookie sheet and pat into a rectangle, one-half inch thick. (If dough is too sticky to handle, sprinkle with flour before placing on cookie sheet.)

Make indentations over the surface of the dough, little pockets with your thumb to hold the flavoring. Spread onion and oil from the skillet over the dough. Sprinkle with coarse salt and rosemary. Cover with a clean kitchen towel and let rise in a warm place for 30 minutes.

Bake the focaccia about 25 minutes. If you managed to find a plastic spray bottle, mist the dough with cold water three times during the first 15 minutes for a crispier crust.

Serving Suggestion

If you're still angry when you're done in the kitchen, eat by yourself. Arguing with someone will make you agitated—not a good condition for your body to be in when you eat. Your digestion shuts down under stress, it's part of the fight or flight response.

But if the physical activity was effective, invite the person you've been in conflict with to break bread with you and share a glass of wine and calmly talk about how you can resolve your differences.

When you confront someone, use words like, "I felt that…" rather than words like, "You always…" You'll get through more effectively.

cooling

Cooling-Off Cold Grapefruit Soufflé

Whipping egg whites is another culinary excuse to transform anger into energy.

You can beat egg whites with an electric mixer, but it is immensely satisfying to use an unlined copper bowl and a wire whisk. The whites achieve maximum volume, you work off your aggression, and you feel as kitchen-competent as Julia Child.

Also, grapefruit contains pectin, as well as vitamin C, potassium, calcium, and iron. Pectin is a soluble fiber that lowers blood cholesterol, thus undoing some of the bad effects anger has on your body.

Cold soufflés are much easier than hot ones—they can be made ahead of time and kept in the refrigerator—and this one is super-simple. It doesn't have to be unmolded, and it fits inside a standard soufflé dish: no need to fuss with paper collars.

Ingredients

¼ cup water

1 envelope unflavored gelatin

1 6-fluid-ounce can frozen grapefruit
juice concentrate

¾ cup sugar

2 egg whites

a few drops of lemon juice or
vinegar to wipe bowl used to beat
egg whites

1 8-ounce container of low-fat
lemon yogurt

1 16-ounce container of low-fat
cottage cheese

for optional decoration: lemon zest,
fresh raspberries

for an optional sauce: 1 package
frozen raspberries in syrup

Preparation

Measure a quarter cup cold water into a small measuring pitcher, empty the envelope of gelatin into it and stir with a fork. Set aside for 15 minutes.

Meanwhile, beat the egg whites. It's easier to separate the eggs when they're cold, but wait until they come to room temperature to beat. The whites must not contain any egg yolk—start again if the yolks break into the whites as you're separating. A large, deep bowl is best for beating—egg whites can increase up to eight times in volume. Put a little lemon juice or vinegar on a paper towel and rub the inside of the bowl and the wires of the whisk before you begin in order to make sure there's no grease lurking about. Hold the bowl at a slight angle with one hand while you beat furiously with the other, attempting to lift up all the whites with each stroke.

The whites are whipped to the right consistency when you lift the whip and the peak of egg white that forms folds over at the tip.

In a small pan, mix the grapefruit concentrate and sugar. Stir in the softened gelatin and heat until very hot, but turn off the flame before the mixture comes to a boil. Stir until it no longer feels gritty.

simmer

Cool off by sharing a dish of cold soufflé and a cookie with a friend who understands. Go somewhere as calm and peaceful as possible, savor the food, and simmer down. Rather than replay the rage, try to talk with your friend about where your anger really came from, try to move through the emotion to serenity.

Anger is the protective side of hurt.

Let mixture cool and thicken, about 15 minutes.

In a blender or food processor, blend the cottage cheese and yogurt together. Pour into a large bowl, add the grapefruit mixture and combine. Then fold in the egg white carefully and gently so it doesn't deflate too much.

Pour this into an 8-inch soufflé dish and refrigerate for at least 2 hours.

Make it fancy by topping with curls of lemon zest, or decorating with fresh raspberries. Or make a sauce to serve with the soufflé: just purée a box of frozen raspberries in the blender, strain if you hate the seeds. Serve in a small pitcher.

down

Crabby

You probably think you're in a bad mood "for no reason"—but, in fact, there always is a reason. When you lash out at an innocent bystander—you snap at the bank teller, for example, or kick the cat—that's transference. You're transferring what you feel about yourself onto other people, trying to get them to carry some of the annoyance for you because it's too painful to carry it all yourself.

If you can stand it, a little reframing works wonders. Pollyanna was a pro at this: the art of putting a positive spin on your problems. You're waiting in line? Instead of considering it a waste of time, enjoy the ten-minute time-out to do a crossword or chat with the people in front of you, to improve your posture, or to read a trashy magazine.

Crabbiness also can be caused by too much external stimuli. You may not even be aware how much your mood is affected by small irritations. Are you someone who can tune out distractions easily—you can have the TV on in the background and learn Greek at the same time—or do unnessary distractions make you crazy? We all vary in the amount of aggravation we can tolerate. Too much unwanted noise

Always, always acquiesce to your own whims, especially when there's no reason not to do so. Want to walk back a block and check out a shoe store when you're in no pressing hurry? Do it. You'll be surprised how your satisfaction with life rises when you regularly indulge yourself like this.

makes your heart beat faster, and can cause your pulse and blood pressure to rise.

If you're feeling overwhelmed, rather than active and alert, there's a three-way solution. First, lower the stimulus level in your immediate environment (for example, wear headphones at the office to shut out the voice of a fellow worker who can talk for hours without coming up for air); second, increase the pleasure of your surroundings (choose a more cheerful room in which to work, clean an area that's causing you visual stress, get yourself a cup of coffee); and third, increase your control over life (make lists, ask the kids to cooperate, plan your day).

It works the other way, too: if you're feeling blah doing something boring like washing up, you can crank up the stimulus level by turning on the radio.

When a crabby mood strikes, you may feel compelled to call a friend. But don't be a bore. Get your whining out of the way quickly so you can proceed directly to the fun stuff, like gossip, sooner. Only ask for advice if you're ready to make an effort to change. In fact, make it a rule that after you have each whined about something, you won't mention it again until you've solved the problem—this way you make time for newer and more interesting whining sessions.

The cure for irritation is a big, greedy helping of indulgence, but not necessarily a food indulgence. Try to make it something that makes you feel good about yourself.

For example, during the day, drink eight glasses of water (being even a little dehydrated can make you tired and irritable) from a beautifully designed crystal goblet that you've bought especially for the purpose. Enjoy being good to your body.

When you're crabby, cosset yourself for a while, then tell yourself to snap out of it.

Try This First

Find a book that makes you laugh out loud now, and assemble a folder filled with funny clippings and cartoons for the future. When you laugh, your blood pressure, heart rate, and muscle tension all drop, circulation improves, and you take in more oxygen. Plus, it's fun.

It may seem silly, but it helps to take notes when something makes you growl. If you track your irritability for a few days, patterns will start to emerge.

Thought to Chew on in the Kitchen

Have I made a habit of being irritable? How one feels about oneself throughout the day is life itself.

Pink Salmon in Foil to Foil a Blue Mood

The only thing to do with a bad mood is to indulge it: play music that reminds you of the good times while you cook something delicious. Fish is perfect: Omega 3 fatty acids, found in fish oil, have been known to ward off depression, as well as reduce the risk of heart disease. Seafood also contains selenium, a trace mineral that seems to put people in a good mood.

You should be eating fish two or three times a week. If your excuse is that it's "too hard to cook," try these two methods.

Does a loved one have an irritating habit, such as mangling the toothpaste tube? Negotiate. Promise that you'll stop doing whatever he hates most, if he remembers to squeeze from the bottom.

pleasure

11

Ingredients

1 salmon steak per person (A salmon steak is a piece of the fish that has been sliced cross-wise through the body, rather than a fillet which is cut the length of the fish.)

salt and pepper

a piece of fresh ginger root or a lemon for juice

2 tablespoons dry sherry

heavy-duty aluminum foil

canola oil

Preparation

Turn on the oven to 400° F.

Get a ruler and measure the thickness of the fish. You'll cook it 15 minutes for each inch of thickness.

Rip off a piece of foil big enough to wrap the salmon. Lightly rub oil all over the foil. Rinse the piece of fish, shake it dry, and lay it on the center of the foil. Fold up the edges of the foil a little. Sprinkle it with salt, pepper, and lemon juice, or grate some fresh ginger over it and pour on a little puddle of sherry.

Fold up the package securely, put it in a pan, and bake in the middle of the oven for the length of time you calculated.

If fish is still opaque in the middle when you take it out, put it back a few minutes longer.

indulgence

Variation: Crispier Salmon with Olives

Preparation

Put salmon steak in a dish, sprinkle it with chopped olives, salt, rosemary, lemon juice, and olive oil. Let it sit for a half hour while you work on your crabby mood and work up an appetite.

Sear the fish under the broiler—first the top, until it's a luscious caramel color, then the bottom.

Transfer to a serving plate and zap it in the microwave on high for 4 minutes.

Serving Suggestion

Serve the salmon with the Rosy Rice or with a salad, a glass of water with a wedge of lime, and gentle music. After you've eaten, try a change of pace to clear your head. For example, become active and go for a walk if, previously, you were doing something idle, like reading the newspaper.

Ingredients

1 salmon steak

about a tablespoon chopped
   olives

salt

about a tablespoon rosemary
   (fresh is better, dried is ok)

juice of one lemon

1 tablespoon olive oil

Serving Suggestion

Serve Rosy Rice with Pink Salmon in foil on pink dishes with a glass of pink lemonade and strawberry mousse for dessert—silly? Yes, but it's guaranteed to take your mind off whatever is making you crabby, and that's your goal right now.

Rosy Rice

Tomato juice contains lots of lycopene, a disease-fighting antioxidant, and a little fat helps you absorb it. Rice is a low-fat, no-cholesterol complex carbohydrate that contains selenium, which may ward off depression.

Besides, it's hard to be crabby when you're eating a pink meal (brownish orange, actually, but let's not quibble).

Preparation

Heat oil in a saucepan over medium heat and cook onions and carrots until they begin to soften, about 3 minutes.

Spray your kitchen shears with nonstick cooking spray, then use them to cut the apricots into small pieces.

Add rice, ginger, salt, stock, tomato juice, and apricots. Bring to a boil. Reduce heat until liquid is just simmering and cover. Cook for 15 to 20 minutes, giving the mixture a stir every few minutes so it doesn't stick to the bottom of the pan. Rice is ready when the liquid has been absorbed and rice is tender.

Ingredients

1 tablespoon olive oil

1 small onion, chopped

½ cup diced carrots

1 cup long-grain rice

¼ teaspoon ground ginger

¼ teaspoon salt

1¼ cups chicken stock

1 cup tomato juice

½ cup dried apricots

nonstick cooking spray

Depressed

Depression goes far deeper than occasional melancholy.

If what you're feeling is just the blahs, rather than soul-numbing depression, you might as well enjoy it. It's not absolutely imperative to feel wonderful constantly. Wallow a while. But how can you tell if you're really depressed or just "moody"? If you have several of the following symptoms nearly every day, all day, for at least two weeks, it's time to get help:

- Helplessness and pessimism
- Sleep problems
- Eating too much or too little
- Social withdrawal
- Feelings of worthlessness
- Inability to concentrate
- Alcohol or drug abuse

If you are seriously depressed, find a therapist—don't try to snap out of it by yourself. Depression can be caused by many different things, from hormone imbalances to genetic predisposition. You're

Be kind to yourself. Nurture the you that's feeling vulnerable right now with good food, kind words, and little treats. Make things as nice for yourself as you would for those you love.

joy

15

not alone—some of the most intelligent and famous people in the world have this problem.

But if there's a possibility that this will pass—if you're mourning a loss or weathering painful circumstances—your only task is to bring yourself through the experience safely.

Look after yourself. What time of day is it? When did you last eat? How much sleep have you been getting? All these things can affect your mood and energy level. If you are very depressed you might miss the signals your body is using to tell you to slow down, take it easy, and eat properly.

Make use of all your senses to heal the hurt you are feeling.

There's something very soothing about touch. If you can't find someone to give you a back rub, or even just hold hands, put on your softest sweater, your worn-until-it's-tissue-paper-thin T-shirt, or wear real silk against your skin. Or take a bath and use your full array of favorite feel-good lotions.

Get outside and commune with nature. Scientists believe we are hard-wired to feel safe and soothed gazing at a vast, predatorless view. The more you are connected with nature, the more you are connected with yourself—it's a calming, centering touchstone. And sunlight is a natural pick-me-up, too.

The feelings that are aroused by fragrance are strong and direct. Odors travel directly to the hypothalamus, main regulator of stress functions, such as blood pressure, heart rate, and neurochemicals. Which smells make you feel comforted? Aromas from the kitchen that you associate with happiness in childhood can be immensely soothing. Go ahead, bake up a storm.

Music can act as a mood-altering drug. It's not the lyrics that soothe, it's the rhythm. Therapists call it the isomodic principle. Use

Drink, drugs, or desserts may lift a bad mood temporarily, but later, you'll feel worse than before.

energy

it to feel better: first play music that matches your existing mood—heavy metal?—then gradually change to songs that have good associations for you until the tempo reflects the kind of mood you'd like to be in. Go from music with percussion, accented beats and rhythm, for example, to something with a slow tempo like classical music with stringed instruments or woodwinds.

The best ways of finding comfort are in feelings of being understood (talk to a friend); being safe (retreat to your room); remembering happy times in the past (look at photos); and being connected to something outside yourself (read).

Try This First

Change your perspective. Lie on the floor on your back—you'll feel weightless, yet connected to the supportive ground. Life seems larger. This is especially effective outside. Watch the clouds. And tonight, look at the stars. They have a wonderful knack of showing you how insignificant everything you're worrying about really is.

If you want to cry, do so. You'll feel better afterwards. If you are afraid of tears, you're afraid of your own emotions, but there is no need to be. Until you fully feel your own pain, you won't be able to let go of it.

No-Regrets Chocolate Pudding

The way we perceive events is as important as the events themselves.

Chocolate makes you feel good because cocoa contains phenylethylamine—a compound apparently released in the brain at times of emotional arousal and said to resemble the effect of falling in love. Chocolate also contains phenols, antioxidants that have been shown to reduce heart disease, and the stimulants theobromine and caffeine, that may boost your levels of serotonin, a natural antidepressant.

Making this pudding is like making mud pies, but when you take it out of the oven, it has miraculously transformed itself into a pudding with a cakey top and sauce underneath. And because there are no eggs or chocolate (cocoa has less fat than chocolate) it's not a dietary disaster.

soothing

Ingredients

1 cup all-purpose flour

¾ cup sugar

¾ cup good quality unsweetened cocoa powder (not the kind of chocolate-milk powder you use for making drinks)

2 teaspoons baking powder

½ teaspoon baking soda

¼ teaspoon ground ginger

¼ teaspoon salt

½ cup skim milk

¼ cup canola oil

1 teaspoon vanilla

½ cup packed dark-brown sugar

1½ cups boiling water

no regrets

Preparation

Preheat the oven to 350° F. Grease a 7-inch square baking dish.

Sift the flour, sugar, one-half cup cocoa, baking powder, baking soda, ginger, and salt into a large bowl. Stir in milk, oil, and vanilla to make a thick batter. Spread in prepared baking dish.

Sprinkle the other quarter cup of cocoa and the brown sugar over the batter in the pan. Pour boiling water over the top—*don't* mix it in!

Put the whole mess in the oven and bake at 350° F for 25 minutes until the sides are set but the middle looks loose. Cool in the pan for five minutes. Serve warm. Try to resist eating the whole thing.

Serving Suggestion

Have a glass of milk with a plate of warm No-Regrets Chocolate Pudding. Calcium has been found to reduce premenstrual mood swings and sadness, as well as build strong bones. And, warmth makes foods more comforting. Curl up in your favorite chair with a blanket, a teddy bear, a book from your childhood, and some pudding.

Comforting Salmon Bake
Like Mother Used to Make

Salmon is a great source of Omega-3 oils (which raise your levels of the feel-good neurotransmitter serotonin), and they don't diminish with the canning process. People suffering from depression often have low levels of selenium, and fish contains that, too.

This is a lighter version of the canned-soup-for-sauce casserole that was popular in the 1950s. Easy to make, and it still tastes good.

Force yourself through the motions of life and have faith that soon its meaning will be restored.

comforting

calming

Preparation

Cook macaroni the way the package tells you. Meanwhile, heat the soup and milk in a saucepan until smooth. Remove from heat and add the ricotta. Combine the macaroni and soup mixture with salmon, celery, onions, and green pepper, and mix well.

Pour into a 1½-quart casserole dish. Bake at 350° F, uncovered, for 30 minutes.

Serving Suggestion

A green salad goes well with the Salmon Bake. And after you've eaten, go for a walk. Just getting out of the house, away from your own little world, can help. Like meditation, the act of walking can take you out of yourself, help you get centered.

Regular exercise causes your body to produce the same good mood endorphins as food.

Ingredients

8 ounces elbow macaroni, uncooked

1 10¾-ounce can reduced-fat cream of celery soup

½ cup skim milk

½ cup low-fat ricotta cheese

1 14¾-ounce can of water-packed salmon, any kind except chum salmon, drained (The softened bones are a good source of calcium, but pick them out if you don't like the crunch.)

1 cup sliced celery

⅓ cup chopped green onions

¼ cup chopped green bell pepper

"It's all right to have butterflies in your stomach. Just get them to fly in formation."

—Dr. Rob Gilbert

Worried

In *Through the Looking Glass*, by Lewis Carroll, the Red Queen advises Alice to do her worrying in advance so that when real trouble comes along, she'll be ready to deal with it. And in fact, good worry helps you prepare for the future—you can figure out solutions to problems and think about the consequences of your actions. Worry becomes negative when it paralyzes you, when it becomes an end in itself. It's important to understand that crises and problems don't make you worry—worry is something you do to yourself.

Women who make a career of obsessive, chronic worry create their own built-in diversion, perhaps to absolve themselves from making the effort of looking for happiness. Worry has become comfortingly familiar, a suit of armor to guard themselves from real problems.

If your negative attitude has become a habit that prevents you from enjoying life, know that it's a habit that can be changed. You can train yourself to be a more positive person by correcting the behavior over and over again until it becomes automatic. Some therapists suggest wearing a rubber band on your wrist to give yourself a little sting every

Maybe you've inherited worry. If your mother was constantly anxious, she may have passed on the idea that a good mother is one who never stops worrying.

time you find yourself fretting or ruminating over painful experiences. Then take some deep breaths and consciously replace the self-defeating thoughts.

Whenever negative thoughts surface, tell yourself you won't address them until your next worry session. Then plan to take short, regular worry sessions when all you do is worry—but that's your quota for the day. (Set a timer for 10 minutes, and go somewhere out of the way, so you won't associate worry with your daily environment. Do this at the same time every day, but not near bedtime.) During these sessions, worry constructively: get the facts, think of every possible outcome, make a plan, write out steps to take. Don't use this time to blame yourself. You need to be able to mull over difficulties in your mind calmly to be able to resolve them—and it really helps if you are on your own side.

You can gain a new perspective on your problem by trying some distancing techniques: write a letter to someone, explaining the situation in detail, from the beginning. It will force you to explore your feelings. Or describe the problem as if it was happening to someone else. Think, too, of how someone you admire would deal with this issue.

Examine each worry to make sure it's legitimate. A friend gave you an angry look and you convinced yourself you did something to make her annoyed—until, a few days later, you realize she had an upset stomach. Your imagination created a problem that hasn't happened. Are there other situations your mind is calling terrible that really aren't?

Maybe it's a decision that's worrying you. Try free-associating on paper. Write down your first thought. Draw a circle around it. Write down the thoughts that spin off from that first thought and link them with lines. Keep going, writing down whatever comes to mind. And focus on what the decision represents: security versus freedom, for

Pain is what you feel, suffering is what you tell yourself you feel.

explore

example. If you articulate a choice in terms of values rather than actions, you can gain a clearer idea of the pros and cons.

If it's a decision between A or B—find alternative C. Maybe there's a compromise or totally different option that you've been blind to because you've been concentrating on A or B.

Your intuition can be a good guide, too. Is your body tense—stomach clenched and jaw tightened—when you think of one alternative, is it more relaxed when you think of the other?

Don't forget, once your daily worry session is over, to feel the bliss of freedom until tomorrow.

Constructive planning feels good, worry doesn't.

Try This First

It's very liberating to make a list of everything that's troubling you, then to ask yourself which of these four categories a particular worry falls into:

- important and controllable
- important and uncontrollable
- unimportant and controllable
- unimportant and uncontrollable

You'll see immediately what problems you can, and should, do something about. A problem well-defined is half-solved.

Worrying may make you feel you're in control, but endless brooding never fixes a situation. Exercise—hard—to distract yourself. It's impossible to be anxious and exhausted at the same time.

constructive

Thought to Chew on in the Kitchen

What's the absolute worst that can happen? Pursue this thought to its most irrational extreme.

cool

Cool as a Cucumber Soup

If you get plenty of calcium when you're young, you'll have one less thing to worry about when you're older! Lack of calcium (found in dairy products like yogurt and sour cream) can lead to loss of bone density and fractures. Calcium also helps regulate blood pressure, nerve transmission, blood clotting, and secretion of hormones and digestive enzymes. Calcium has been found to calm PMS symptoms, too.

Preparation

Blend everything in the blender, add salt and pepper as necessary, chill in the refrigerator, and eat within a few hours of preparing.

Serving Suggestion

Eating a food rich in vitamin D (like fish or eggs) together with calcium enhances its effects, which makes tuna salad a good accompaniment for cucumber soup.

If it's a hot day, borrow an idea from the Japanese and offer each person around the dining table a damp washcloth that's been stored in the refrigerator. Everyone will find it refreshing to rub on their hands and neck.

Ingredients

1 large cucumber peeled, halved and seeded

½ cup nonfat sour cream

½ cup nonfat yogurt

1 cup nonfat chicken broth (If you only have the regular kind, strain it to take out all the fat globules which won't dissolve, because this soup is served cold.)

½ cup fresh mint or cilantro (either will do, but don't use both) with the leaves stripped from the stems

optional: salt and pepper

25

possibilities

Remedial Raisin Oatmeal Cookies

If you don't eat much meat and you feel depressed and tired, as well as worried, consider the possibility that your diet might be deficient in iron. Raisins are a concentrated source of many minerals—including iron.

There is no refined version of oatmeal, so it retains all its goodness: the B vitamins, linoleic acid, and vitamin E. Oatmeal is a nerve restorative and sedative.

Why are negative thoughts so dangerous? Because by repeating something over and over, you make it true—it's called self-hypnosis!

steps

Ingredients

¾ cup sugar

2 tablespoons butter
(Don't substitute anything for
the butter. Nothing else makes
cookies as delicious.)

1 large egg

2 tablespoons skim milk

¼ cup applesauce

¾ cup all-purpose flour

¼ teaspoon baking soda

½ teaspoon each cinnamon
and nutmeg

¼ teaspoon salt

1¼ cup quick-cooking oatmeal
(not instant)

½ cup raisins (They should be
fresh and soft. Dry raisins will
absorb moisture from the
cookie dough, making the
resulting cookies dry.)

Preparation

Preheat oven to 350° F.

Beat the sugar and butter together in an electric mixer until smooth and creamy. Add the egg, milk, and applesauce, and mix until smooth.

In a separate bowl, sift flour, soda, cinnamon, nutmeg, and salt. Add dry ingredients gradually to the creamed mixture and stir until blended.

Add oats and raisins, Mix.

Drop the dough by rounded teaspoons onto a lightly floured cookie sheet.

Bake for 10 to 13 minutes at 350° F until lightly browned.

Makes about 24 cookies

Serving Suggestion

Drink a glass of milk with a cookie (or two, or three), warm from the oven. The combination still has the filling, soothing properties it did when you came home from grade school.

"It is hard to fight an enemy who has an outpost in your head."

—Sally Kempton

Self-Critical

Putting yourself down is an emotional bad habit you may not realize you have. Even when you recognize what you're doing, it's incredibly difficult to stop.

But you must make the effort not to criticize yourself. If you can't feel at peace and comfortable with yourself, you can never be truly happy. You wouldn't want to live in a house where someone was constantly finding fault with you, and you shouldn't live in a body where you never allow yourself to feel loved. When you become aware of what you're telling yourself and the destructive effect it has, you'll make the effort to stop.

The idea of loving yourself may seem very self-centered and selfish, unless you've come across the concept of the "child within." This theory maintains that you should treat yourself as you would a small, innocent child, and love her in the same way. Applaud her when she does something right—encourage her, for example, in a healthy lifestyle—and try to understand her motives when she does something "wrong."

Where does that harsh critic come from? That voice is your mother, your teachers, the kids from grade school, a tangled chorus you paid attention to way back when. Your mind is trying to protect you from criticism today by recreating those voices—making sure it's the first to get in with any negative comments that might be made about your behavior.

Be good to yourself every day, don't wait until you feel desperately in need of a psychic hug. At the very least, show yourself the same kindness and courtesy you show strangers.

And part of being good to yourself is choosing healthy things to eat. Not caring about your body is one of the biggest put-downs you can do to yourself.

If there's a specific incident from your past that you can't let go of, it often helps to devise a penance for yourself. If you deeply regret not spending time with your grandmother when she was alive, assign yourself a year of Saturdays volunteering at an aging-people's home.

If beating yourself up has become a bad habit, conquering the inner critic will take persistence. How do you give it up? First, decide what method you're going to use to pull yourself up every time you criticize yourself. The next step is to tell yourself, "Stop." You will have to keep doing this over and over again. (Changing a bad habit takes constant repetition and exposure—that's how advertisements work.) Then you must exchange the negative statements with positive, self-supportive statements. And mean them!

When you stop blaming others, your education has started. When you stop blaming yourself, your education is complete.

Try This First

Self-talk is usually so automatic you don't notice it. The first step is simply to notice every time you start talking negatively to yourself. You've probably become so used to it you don't even realize you are whipping yourself into a frenzy of stress and perfectionism. Instead of inwardly ranting and raving, describe your thoughts to yourself to be aware of what's really going on in your mind. When someone's late, for example, acknowledge that you're angry at having to wait, and plan what you'll do next.

The only way to lose your self-worth is by saying negative things to yourself.

If you are going to berate yourself when things go wrong, make sure you also recognize and praise yourself when you do something to be proud of.

Give your inner critic a name "Stop that, Petunia!"—so you'll take it less seriously.

Thought to Chew on in the Kitchen

I'm terrific—aren't I? Brag about yourself—then have an argument with that carping little voice in your head that immediately tries to tear you down.

Gingerbread with a Kick

The only thing in your life that should deliver a kick is this dense, dark bread with the kick of ginger and molasses. Molasses contains vitamin E, which helps slow aging and keeps your heart healthy.

Serving Suggestion

This gingerbread is wonderful served warm from the oven with vanilla yogurt. It seems like a dessert, but you can eat it at any meal. Try it for breakfast. There's no law that says a food only can be eaten at one time of day. Ask your body what it feels like—and don't criticize if it feels like dessert for breakfast.

be good to yourself

Ingredients

1 cup brown sugar (or white, if that's all you have, it doesn't really matter)

¼ teaspoon salt

2 teaspoons ground ginger

½ teaspoon ground cinnamon

½ teaspoon cloves

1 cup canola oil

1 cup molasses

2 teaspoons baking soda

1 cup strong, very hot coffee— instant or brewed (replace with hot water if you're trying to keep your caffeine intake low)

2½ cups all-purpose flour

2 eggs, well-beaten

recognize

Preparation

Preheat oven to 350° F. Grease two 5x9-inch baking pans.

In a large bowl, combine sugar, salt, ginger, cinnamon, and cloves. Stir in oil, then molasses, combine well.

Combine baking soda and hot coffee, and immediately stir into molasses mixture. Stir in eggs. There's a lot of stirring in this recipe, as you may have noticed. Be as vigorous as you like, until you get to the next step.

Stir flour into liquid mixture gradually to prevent lumping, don't over-mix—just stir until dry ingredients are blended.

Pour into prepared pans. (This bread rises! Fill the pans only halfway.)

Bake for 40 to 45 minutes, or until a knife inserted in the center comes out clean and the cake begins to pull away from the sides. Sinking in the middle is normal. (Just as expanding in the middle is normal for the rest of us.)

Highly Acclaimed Low-Fat Hummus

Beans, peas, and lentils are a good source of protein, which is essential for proper brain-cell communication, attention span, and mental ability.

This dip is highly acclaimed because it's much lower in fat than the traditional recipe, but tastes just as good.

Preparation

Combine everything in the blender, putting the liquids in first. Process until smooth. Add salt if needed.

Serving Suggestion

Hummus and pita bread make a complete protein combination. Take a bite in front of a mirror. It'll give you something else to be self-critical about—until you realize that before you is an ordinary human being doing what human beings do. Make a silly face at her. Let her be.

applaud

Ingredients

juice of one lemon

¾ cup fat-free plain yogurt

1 19-ounce can of chickpeas, drained, but not really thoroughly

2-4 cloves of garlic, depending on how much you like garlic

salt

optional: 1 teaspoon toasted sesame seed oil

Meditation is a good way of separating yourself from your critical voices.

32

variety

Bored

You're apathetic about everything, tired, and uninterested. This sounds a lot like depression, and maybe it is, if you often feel this way.

Like depression, boredom can be a mood your mind hides behind so you don't have to feel emotions you don't want to let yourself feel.

Or maybe you feel bored because you're deprived of your hectic routine. But this is a time to recharge—completely valid and necessary, especially if you work in a demanding, people-intensive environment.

If you're feeling bored, your diet is probably boring, too. Ever tasted pomegranates, rhubarb, Jerusalem artichokes, starfruit, quinoa, amaranth? There are dozens of fruits, vegetables, and grains you've probably never tried. Varying your food choices provides you with a much wider range of nutrients that are important for your health. Experiment with a completely new-to-you food every week. Explore Asian supermarkets and Indian delis. Turn food shopping into an adventure rather than a chore.

Stuck inside because of the weather or an illness? Now is your opportunity to cook a really elaborate meal, plan a sewing project, or make valentines.

Go out on a limb. That's where the sweetest fruit is.

Destructive behavior doesn't work. Using drugs or alcohol increases the numb feelings, obscuring the real problem.

33

adventure
excitement

Try This First

Take a piece of paper and write, "What I really, really want." Spend at least an hour making a list. No editing, no crossing out. Just take dictation.

Wheel the TV into the bathroom to watch while you soak in a bath. Read a novel. Or devote a whole weekend to self-restoration of the face-mask and pedicure kind.

When you're refreshed, it's time to stir things up. Surprise yourself. Skip town. Use up those frequent-flier miles. Paint the walls blue. Go blond. Try something you're afraid of. Any shift in perspective is energizing—an adventure is an inconvenience looked at in a different way.

Each of us is writing the story of our own journey through life. The plot can be dull, flat, and dreary, or it can be full of twists, turns, and excitements. Your call. Every line, every location, every adventure is written by you.

Be enthusiastic about life. Grab hold of it—take it with gusto, with pleasure, with appreciation. The world is a banquet full of magical things patiently waiting for you to come to your senses.

If everyone around you seems boring—guess what! Yes, you're the one with the problem.

Thought to Chew on in the Kitchen

What am I trying to protect myself from? Somehow, somewhere, you were once hurt during your pursuit of fun and adventure. You gave up in order to avoid more pain and wrapped yourself in ennui for protection.

Carrot Salad Surprise

Carrots are a great source of beta-carotene, one of the essential antioxidant nutrients that lowers your risk of heart disease, cancer, cataracts, and arthritis. And, studies have found that thinking ability, memory, and concentration stay high through life when you eat lots of beta-carotene–rich foods.

The surprise is how orange juice and apple enhance the taste of carrots.

Preparation

Combine all ingredients in a salad bowl.

Serving Suggestion

Carrot salad makes a piquant counterpoint to heavier salads like potato or lentil. If you keep batches of several salads on hand you can serve them with cold chicken or deli cuts for easy summer meals. Beat boredom by eating this picnic-style meal anywhere other than the dining room or kitchen!

Ingredients

4 small carrots, scraped and grated or shredded in a food processor (Smaller carrots are sweeter and more tender. Avoid the cracked ones with lots of tiny rootlets. Choose the brightest orange.)

I Red Delicious apple, grated

½ cup dried currants

juice of one medium orange (Fresh-squeezed orange juice works best.)

2 tablespoons carrot juice

I tablespoon fresh grated ginger

magic

Unusual Lentil Salad

Parsnips are high in potassium and folic acid. Deficiency in folic acid, a B vitamin, causes depression—and it's one of the most common deficiencies in the United States. Lethargy often results from a lack of iron in the diet—lentils have lots of iron.

Bored with your usual green salad? This is unusual and delicious. Make it early in the day and let it come to room temperature.

Serving Suggestion

This lentil salad can substitute for the usual potatoes or rice you'd serve with a chicken or meat dish. As you eat it, savor the unusual flavors. When you're bored, eating can become an automatic way to fill the emotional void. To stop falling into that rut, pay attention to every mouthful.

Ingredients

3 cups water

1 cup brown lentils (Scrutinize the lentils carefully to make sure no pebbles have been included.)

1 large carrot, peeled and cut into rounds

1 parsnip, peeled and cut in rounds; cut larger rounds in half (These are the roots that look like white carrots.)

½ onion, chopped

½ cup chopped cilantro

3 cups chopped celery stalks

4 ounces feta cheese, crumbled into small chunks

Dressing:

8 tablespoons best quality virgin olive oil

1 tablespoon lemon juice

1 teaspoon salt

All you need is within you.

journey

Preparation

Combine water, lentils, carrots, parsnips, and onion in a large saucepan. Bring to a boil, then lower heat and simmer, covered, for 20 minutes. How much water is absorbed depends on the age of the lentils. You could drain all the liquid off, once everything is done. (Test a lentil, poke a knife in a chunk of parsnip to make sure it's tender.) But it's easier to go on cooking until all the water is absorbed. (If there is excess liquid, it makes this dish more of a vegetable stew and less of a salad, but that's not necessarily a bad thing.)

While the lentils are cooking, whisk the dressing ingredients together in a large salad bowl. When the lentils are done and have cooled, add them to the dressing in the salad bowl. Add cilantro, celery, and feta cheese. Toss everything together.

Feeling Old

Do you get the birthday blues? Every year do you expect to feel loved and celebrated and fêted the way you were when Mom provided cake, ice cream, lots of presents, and attention?

The only way to make sure you have the kind of birthday party you want is to plan it yourself. If you want pink frosting, find the pinkest and gooiest. Tell people exactly the kind of pampering you want, how you want them to make a fuss. Invite everyone over, even if it's just for a slice of cake. Embrace the ritual. Don't wait for someone else to validate you, do it for yourself.

Some of the process of getting old is good and some is not. But it's what happens. There are compromises and trade-offs to be made. Becoming invisible—and you will—is a shock. Society admires youth and beauty. You could learn to roll with the punches, but why not study them, think about them, and defy the stereotypes?

And there are rewards: a better sense of self, freedom from competition. You lose the adolescent angst, become more sure of yourself, more in control of your own life.

You can use that nagging sense of time running out while you're falling short of your promise and your goals to prod yourself to further accomplishment. Just don't fall into the trap of comparison.

Celebrate your birthday with some doddery old geezer a few years older than yourself. It's guaranteed to make you feel like a teenager.

embrace

Every decade, do some serious thinking about the previous ten years and the ten years ahead, not just to mourn the goals you haven't reached and places you haven't been, but to plan and dream. Your definitions of success and happiness change. Every decade, you have a different world view. This is the way to create a life you can look back at with satisfaction.

What do you no longer have patience for? What do you want to achieve while there's still time? What did you wish for last year when you blew out the candles on your birthday cake? Did it come true? Can you make it come true before your next birthday?

When you create an itinerary for your life, the way becomes less scary, the points of interest along the way are something to look forward to, not feared.

The older you get, the fewer people there are to push you around.

The older you get, the fewer excuses you have to waste time with people or events that don't interest you.

Happy Birthday Carrot Cake

There's a growing consensus among scientists that aging is due to free radical reactions. Free radicals enter the body in cigarette smoke, fried foods, and smog—and we generate them ourselves when we're stressed. The body produces natural antioxidants to neutralize the damage, but it can't produce enough. Years of free radical attacks contribute to gradual loss of memory and thinking.

An excellent reason to make sure you eat antioxidant nutrients—vitamins C and E and beta-carotene, found in carrots—is to avoid being accelerated into old age!

This carrot cake is moist and fruity. Best of all, it's good on non-birthdays, too.

Let your inner teeny-bopper act out. Crank up the music. Run through the water sprinkler in the summer. Jump rope. See if anyone remembers how to play jacks.

celebrate

party

Ingredients

- 1 16-ounce can of crushed pineapple in unsweetened juice
- 1 pound carrots (Do not grate carrots ahead of time because they dry out)
- 2¼ cups flour
- 1 teaspoon baking soda
- ¾ teaspoon salt
- ¾ teaspoon nutmeg
- ½ teaspoon baking powder
- ½ teaspoon cinnamon
- ¼ teaspoon cloves
- 1 cup sugar
- ⅓ cup canola oil
- 2 large eggs
- 1 8-ounce jar of puréed baby food carrots
- 1½ cups raisins
- 1 generous cup pecan pieces, toasted and coarsely chopped

Frosting:

- 2 cups confectioners' sugar
- 1 tub (8 oz) light cream cheese at room temperature

Preparation

Preheat oven to 350° F. Grease a 10-inch springform pan.

Set pineapple to drain and grate carrots.

Sift together flour, baking soda, salt, nutmeg, baking powder, cinnamon, and cloves.

Beat sugar and oil in large mixing bowl at medium speed until blended. Add the eggs, scraping side and bottom of bowl after each addition. Add the baby food carrots.

At low speed, beat in dry ingredients just until combined. By hand, mix in the raisins, carrots, pecans, and pineapple.

Pour into the pan, bake at 350° F for 75 minutes, until a knife inserted in center of cake comes out clean. Let sit in oven until cool. (Don't try to cover with frosting until the cake is completely cool.)

Beat frosting ingredients together with electric mixer, then spread over cake.

Serving Suggestion

Cake plus champagne equals a party, no matter what day it is. Think up an excuse, gather some friends, and pop open some bubbly.

Sprightly Spinach Quiche

Dietary fat is a prime generator of free radicals, the unstable molecules that contribute to the signs of aging in our bodies. With a low-fat diet full of fruit and vegetables—preferably eight or more servings a day of foods like orange juice, strawberries, spinach, and broccoli—and a daily exercise routine, you can prevent premature aging.

People who eat greens such as spinach or kale a few times a week lower their risk of macular degeneration—the most common cause of blindness after age sixty-five.

Spinach provides a good serving of magnesium, too. Lack of magnesium can cause depression, irritability, and mood swings.

This is a crustless quiche—the easiest kind.

Serving Suggestion

Since eating a vitamin C–rich food together with iron-rich foods, like spinach, increases iron absorption, have a glass of orange juice with the quiche. Share your meal with someone your own age, talk about what you like about getting older.

share

Ingredients

1 10-ounce package frozen chopped spinach

3 tablespoons nonfat dry milk powder

2 eggs

1 15-ounce container of nonfat ricotta cheese

1 4.4 ounce packet of flavored light cheese, like Boursin

Preparation

Grease a 9-inch pie plate with nonfat cooking spray.

Put the frozen spinach in a microwave-safe container. (Don't add water, no matter what it might say on the packet.) Cook on *high* for about 3 minutes, interrupting it occasionally to break up the solid icy bits.

Place the spinach in a saucepan. Cook over medium heat until most of the moisture has cooked away—2 or 3 minutes. Add the milk powder and stir until it has been absorbed.

Add the Boursin cheese and stir until there are no lumps of cheese. Turn off the heat.

In a small bowl, beat the eggs with a fork, and add them to the spinach mixture, then add the ricotta.

Stir to combine, then pour the mixture into the pie plate.

Bake in 350° F oven for about 40 minutes, or until the edges have started to brown and the center is firm and doesn't wobble when you move the pan.

As you get older, you have to give up the struggle to stay youthful and adored. If you spend your life seeking applause, you're not paying attention to your own inner needs and desires.

> "To love oneself is the beginning of a lifelong romance."
>
> —Oscar Wilde

Low Self-Esteem

It's a lot easier to blame someone else rather than take responsibility for making ourselves feel better. But as adults, we either ask for, or allow other people, to treat us as they do. And by allowing something, you reinforce it.

Self-esteem is your decision to treat yourself as a beloved friend: that means respecting yourself, taking care of yourself, nurturing yourself. Get a haircut, get a manicure, pamper yourself with a facial. Buy a plant. Rearrange your furniture, or, on a smaller scale, tidy up your desk. You deserve to live in nice surroundings.

Face up to what needs to be faced. Just taking the first step toward solving a problem will make you feel better about yourself.

Look at photos of yourself as a child. Remember learning to ride a bicycle? Eating in a fancy restaurant? You've accomplished so much over the years—and you were such a cute kid!

Watching television can actually lower your self-esteem. Get involved with something that stretches your mind instead. Master something new—a computer program, soufflés, speaking in public.

Spending time doing things you are good at immediately boosts your self-esteem. Finish the crossword puzzle, bake brownies, beat someone at Monopoly.

learning

Nothing makes you feel better about yourself than a new accomplishment. Keep adding new successes, no matter how small.

Try This First

Exercise can be tremendously empowering. Not only because aerobic exercise increases mood-boosting endorphins while you're doing it, but also because when you get physically strong, you're so much more confident in all areas of your life.

Own your successes. Celebrate the small things. Open a bottle of wine when you make a perfect soufflé. Women don't often brag, but it's important. It makes you feel good and it spurs you on to do better things.

To help you put things in perspective, make a list of the things you do well—you can actually program a VCR, you're never late for anything, you balance your checkbook every month.

empower

Looking Good Pumpkin Soup

Looking good is a big part of self-esteem, and antioxidant nutrients help by slowing the aging process in your cells. One of the most powerful antioxidants is beta-carotene, found in pumpkin and sweet potatoes.

Peanut butter contains choline, which is converted in the brain to a nerve chemical that's important for memory and general mental functioning—low levels are common in old people.

The peanut butter makes this soup deliciously unusual.

Dwelling on your failures is self-defeating. Being down on yourself just drags you further down. You must be your own coach, friend, and cheerleader.

confident

boost

Ingredients

1 large or 2 small sweet potatoes

1 10½-ounce can of chicken broth

6 ounces smooth peanut butter

14 ounces canned pumpkin

skim milk

salt and freshly ground pepper

chives for garnish, if you have them

Preparation

Pierce the sweet potatoes with a fork, and microwave 5 to 7 minutes until they give when you squeeze them with an oven mitt on your hand.

Let the sweet potatoes cool. Squeeze the insides out of the skin and into the blender. Discard the skins. Add the chicken broth and peanut butter, and blend thoroughly until very smooth.

Put this purée in a big cooking pot and add the pumpkin. Add enough milk to make the texture soup-like. Heat through, and season to taste.

Serving Suggestion

Make cute croutons for this soup by cutting slices of stale bread into shapes with little star-shaped cookie cutters. Spray lightly with cooking spray, sprinkle with herbs, and bake in a 400° F oven for 15 minutes. Delight in your own gourmet abilities.

Check in with yourself every day—what do I need right now? What will make me happy today?

freedom

Fearless Flax Bread

The oils in flaxseed and in walnuts are of the Omega-3 type, which have been shown to alleviate depression. These oils also provide essential fatty acids for great skin.

Preparation

Preheat oven to 350° F.

Coat an 8x4-inch loaf pan with nonstick spray.

Beat sugar and eggs together in a large bowl with a mixer until thick and pale. Add the flaxseed meal and sift in the flour, baking powder, baking soda, and salt.

In a separate bowl, combine buttermilk, oil, and vanilla.

Add these ingredients to the flour. Add mixture and mix until just combined.

Stir in walnut pieces.

Pour into pan and bake at 350° F for 55 minutes, or until a knife inserted in the center comes out clean.

Ingredients

¾ cup sugar

2 large eggs

6 tablespoons flaxseed meal (found at health food stores)

2 cups all-purpose flour

1½ teaspoons baking powder

½ teaspoon baking soda

½ teaspoons salt

¾ cup low-fat buttermilk

¼ cup canola oil

1 teaspoon vanilla

1 cup walnut pieces

Serving Suggestion

Just this once, spread something delicious and fattening, like butter or lemon curd spread, on the bread. Food is one of life's pleasures. Give yourself an occasional break. If you eat whole foods that are low in fat and high in fiber 90 percent of the time, you can allow yourself an indulgence 10 percent of the time. It's what you consistently do that matters.

fly away

Feeling Trapped

What's stopping you from getting what you want? Are there concrete, practical obstacles in your way, or are you sabotaging yourself?

If you had a day completely free, what would you most likely do? Dreaming can give you a clue to what's missing in your life. What brings you the most joy? What makes time fly? When does the day drag? What are you doing when you feel really glad to be alive—feeling not just pleasure, but joy?

Whatever it is, you should be doing as much of it as you can. You may be ready to shed an old life and take on a new one.

Think about the best possible existence you could have. How can you make it happen in five years? Make lists, lots of lists—your fears, what it will take to reach your goals, what you want more of in your life, what you must have less of. Listen for the subtle nudging of your subconscious. When you write down your wishes and dreams, they become goals.

Perhaps you gave up the idea of being a teacher, but that doesn't mean you can't find a way of teaching or working with children. There

Think of your goals as feelings. You want to learn about the stock market to feel in control of your finances. When you're tempted to give up, concentrate on that feeling of being in control.

You can always change your goals, but if you don't have any to begin with, you have nothing to aim for.

Visualization is the key to achieving your dreams. If you can picture it—and the more specifically, the better—you can have it.

49

free

are lots of ways to do what you love. Research your favorite subject on the Web, ask a librarian, or find someone who is living the life you'd love to have. Keep following paths, taking small steps, refining your goals.

Your subconscious takes notes. Daydream about being completely successful. Fantasize, a lot, about your ideal occupation. Find a notebook and write down everything that comes to mind. Write about your anguishes, hopes, desires, and wants. Keep a journal that will help you define your goals on paper, making them seem real and doable. It's a place to release stress, too. When you take time to write, you give yourself a time-out to vent and let off steam safely.

It also gives you perspective and helps you to look at events more realistically when you're reviewing your past. The important things in your life will become apparent. You'll have a record of your changing reactions and inner growth.

As former Texas governor Ann Richards has said: "There's no mystery to success. No secret. There is only determination, and keeping on when everyone else has run home to mama."

Try This First

Make a tiny life change—walk to work instead of driving, learn Portuguese—to see how it feels, and to point you in a new direction.

Thought to Chew on in the Kitchen

What helped me attain the goals I've reached so far in life? You can use those resources again and again.

Make-Your-Own-Good-Fortune Cookies

A good fortune cookie prediction is an instant mood lifter—even if you have to resort to making your own!

Make these with a friend, because they need to be folded while they're hot. (If you're by yourself, bake just two at a time, so you can fold them before you make more.)

Open-ended goals don't work. Build in an end result that you want to achieve. Don't just think, "I want to brush up my Italian." Plan to be able to read a specific Italian book by a specific date, and work out the steps you'll need to get to that point.

Dreaming is the most practical activity there is. Nothing happens until you consider the possibilities.

good fortune

51

Preparation

Preheat oven to 350° F. Grease a cookie sheet.

Beat the egg white in a bowl. Add the oil, sugar, instant tea, and flour, beating after each addition.

Take a heaping teaspoonful of batter and drop onto the cookie sheet. Spread it out until it's a thin circle. Keep each cookie about four inches away from another.

Bake about five minutes, or until edges turn golden. Loosen with a spatula. Lay a fortune across the middle, fold the circle in half, press the edges together, and drape over the side of a bowl to make the classic fortune cookie shape. Hold the cookie closed for a moment, then allow to cool.

Cookie sheets must cool between batches. (Use several and alternate them.)

Serving Suggestion

Fortune cookies make a nice little treat to serve anyone going through a decision-making process. Dream up different outcomes for your friend's dilemma, write them on fortunes, and invite her over. Serve with green tea and ginger ice cream.

Ingredients

1 egg white

2 tablespoons canola oil

¼ cup confectioners' sugar

¼ teaspoon instant tea mix

¼ cup all-purpose flour

14 fortunes written on thin strips of paper

day dream

Sea Change Tuna Salad

Magnesium—found in fish—is an effective tranquilizer. Fifty percent of people who have acute migraine headaches have low magnesium.

Preparation

To hard-cook the eggs, start by having them at room temperature, so they won't have a greenish tinge when they're done. Put the eggs in a pan and cover with cold water. Bring the water to a boil, then reduce the heat and simmer for 12 minutes. Rinse immediately under cold water to avoid a greenish ring around the yolk. If the eggs are hard to peel, they were either very fresh eggs or cooked too long.

Mix all the ingredients in a salad bowl.

Serving Suggestion

Scoop tuna salad onto a bed of mesclun salad greens. Use the protein-power you get from the fish to think your way through your goals and options.

Ingredients

1 12-ounce premium albacore solid-packed white tuna, drained (using flaked tuna looks as if you've used cat food)

1 8-ounce jar low-fat mayonnaise

1 16-ounce jar of sweet mixed pickles cut in half or quarters (save liquid for the dressing in the Clean-Out-the-Beans Salad)

1 cup raw long-grain rice, cooked as per package

2 eggs

Unhappy

Do you realize you have a choice here? You can decide to be miserable, or you can decide to be happy.

Why do people get the blues? Because Mother Nature gets us to cooperate with her plan for us (staying alive and procreating) through happiness and pain, and only because neither last. If women never forgot the pain of childbirth, there'd be no more children born. If the joy of reaching a goal lasted, we'd never bother to strive for anything else ever again.

The plus side is that we all come with a capacity to tolerate setbacks and to recover from their effects, and to feel joy all over again.

You can be as happy as you make up your mind to be. You can work on it in two ways. You can figure out what it is that you do to prevent yourself from enjoying life—how and why you sabotage yourself—and you can add happy activities to your day.

Have you been getting enough B vitamins and iron lately? Lack of these can make you feel low. A well-balanced diet is important, too. There are two endorphins that affect our moods—serotonin and

Live in the moment. Use all your senses and live in the moment, the way children and dogs do. Let go, relax, become absorbed in what you're doing. Pay attention to all the little, gentle pleasures of an ordinary day—the feel of the sun in early spring, a phone call from a friend, a warm muffin—they all bring happiness when they're properly appreciated and enjoyed.

norepinephrine. The body makes these feel-good brain chemicals from the foods we eat. So, in theory, you can eat carbohydrates and feel better. However, at the same time you should eat some fiber, so that the food is absorbed more slowly and your blood sugar doesn't rise and fall erratically.

Try This First

Unhappiness comes in two flavors: the lethargic, jaded variety where nothing seems worth doing, and the vicious kind where you're upset and want to throw something. When you are feeling unhappy due to boredom, you need to increase your arousal level. Escapist activities that get you moving are the answer. A list is coming up. When you're angry, relaxing distractions work well. There's a list of these, too.

Happiness is less a matter of getting what you want than of how you feel about what you have.

Get-Glad Suggestions for Lethargic Moods

- Nail some bottle caps to the underneath of an old pair of shoes and start tap dancing.
- Find a friend to go to a sleazy wig store with you and try on different personalities.
- Sing in the shower.
- Make a tape of instant good-mood music.
- Rent a convertible for the weekend.
- Check travel Websites for cheap, last-minute flights.
- Skinny dip.
- Paint or draw something. Forget talent and creating something pretty—art is a way of noticing what you see and studying it by trying to capture what you see on paper.
- Take a dog to the park.
- Rent a tandem bike.
- Fly a kite.
- Put on some dance music and start moving, even if you think you don't feel like it. Nurture your inner teenager—turn up the volume.
- If your favorite store is having a sale, check it out. Snagging a bargain can have a miraculous effect on your mood.
- Visit a fortune-teller.
- Go to the zoo.
- Get a pedicure.
- Get a fake tattoo.
- Have an adventure.
- Serve your staff champagne.
- Move the furniture. Or, on a smaller scale, your desk top. Polish the silver. Anything that changes things for the better and gives fast results.

Know how fortunate you are.
Count your blessings.

- Blow bubbles. Get a kit from a toy store or twist a piece of wire into a circle, dip it in dish-washing liquid and blow out a cascade of fragile rainbow bubbles.
- Treat yourself to breakfast out.
- Browse in a bookstore's humor section.
- Write down a list of splurges and do one each day.
- Pick up fresh flowers for your desk every Monday. Freesias last well and have a wonderful scent. Try different ones until you find your favorite.
- Throw out and replace all your ripped, stained, or elastic-shot underwear. From now on, resolve to wear only lingerie that makes you feel pampered.
- Call dial-a-joke.

Allow for your sources of happiness to change. Maybe you turn to the same pleasure over and over—going to the movies, shopping at the mall. There's so much more.

Get-Glad Suggestions for Angry Moods

- Play Beethoven's Pastoral Symphony, find a chopstick or a knitting needle and start conducting.
- Get out all your nail polish bottles and paint each toenail a different color.
- Put up a bird feeder.
- Find a park that has rowboats for hire.
- Lie in a hammock.
- Get up early and watch the sunrise.
- Buy an ice cream cone and window shop.
- Play with a yo-yo.
- Swing on the swings in a playground.
- Go for a ferry ride.
- Buy a chorus line of windup toys and set them in motion.
- Rediscover a junk food you'd forgotten about.
- Browse through a comic book store and buy your favorites.
- Read a story to a child.
- Get out the good soap and expensive bath oil and use it right now.
- Splurge on some top-quality Beluga and eat it all yourself.
- Tell your journal all about it. Write it all down, every awful detail.
- Curl up with a really trashy novel or magazine.
- Take a nap.
- Give yourself a manicure.
- Shopping can be a form of meditation when you choose a store like a hardware store.
- Take a bus ride. Just sit and watch the world. Eavesdrop. Think about things.
- Look through your photo album, remember the good times—and plan some good times to come.

happy

- Write a letter to a teacher who touched your life in some way.
- Get a massage.
- Spend the whole afternoon at the movies.
- Treat yourself to a facial or day spa.
- If you're at work, take a few little breaks throughout the day to stretch. Walk around the block, take your lunch to the park, buy flowers for your desk, or go to a cosmetic counter and test different scents.

Who taught you about happiness? Someone who led you to believe you need money to be happy? Perhaps you need to define happiness for yourself.

moments

move

Out-of-the-Blues Muffins

Loss of motor function—your agility to do just about anything—is the first part of the brain to deteriorate. That's a depressing thought, until you learn that scientists have found that one of the best foods, along with prunes and raisins, for improving motor skills and memory is blueberries.

And the carbohydrates in the rest of the muffin restore the brain's serotonin, a natural antidepressant.

Preparation

Preheat oven to 400° F.

In a large bowl, sift the flour, baking powder, baking soda, and salt. Add the sugar and mix well.

(You're aiming to mix the wet and dry ingredients together as little as possible, so mix the dry ingredients thoroughly now, while they're dry.)

In a smaller bowl, beat the egg, then add juice, oil, vanilla, and yogurt and mix these wet ingredients well.

Add liquid ingredients to dry ingredients, stirring just until combined.

Fold in the blueberries.

Spoon into muffin cups, bake at 400° F for 18 minutes. Remove muffins from pan as soon as you can handle them, otherwise moisture condenses on the bottom of the cups and they become soggy.

Serving Suggestion

Have a muffin with a cup of coffee. Sit outside if weather permits. Or just sit at the window and watch the world for a moment.

Ingredients

2 cups all-purpose flour

1 teaspoon baking powder

1 teaspoon baking soda

¼ teaspoon salt

⅓ cup sugar

1 egg

¼ cup orange juice

2 tablespoons canola oil

1 teaspoon vanilla extract

1 8-ounce container of vanilla low-fat yogurt

1¾ cups washed blueberries, which is about six ounces by weight. (Measure the blueberries in a Pyrex glass pitcher with the amounts measured on the side, hold it up level to your eye and squint. This recipe was tested with more blueberries, on the theory that you can't have too much of a good thing, but actually you can. The fruit clumps together and the muffins fall apart if you use too much fruit.)

Happiness Is a Cranberry Muffin Hot from the Oven

…and knowing that it's low-fat.

Cranberries have been found to prevent urinary tract infections and contain vitamins C and A and potassium—potassium helps control blood pressure and hypertension.

Preparation

Preheat oven to 400° F.

Spray a 6-cup muffin tin (with 4-inch cups) with cooking spray.

Lightly beat the egg, then mix in the cranberry sauce, sugar, oil, vanilla, and buttermilk.

Sift the flour, baking powder, salt, and cinnamon on top. Fold in the cranberries.

Divide batter between each cup of the muffin tin.

Bake 20 minutes, or until a knife inserted comes out clean.

Serving Suggestion

Adopt the civilized English custom of inviting friends to afternoon tea. Make it a happy occasion by serving cakes, cookies, cranberry muffins, and a choice of fine teas.

Ingredients

1 cup whole berry cranberry sauce (about three quarters of a 16-ounce can)

1 large egg

⅔ cup packed light brown sugar

⅓ cup canola oil

1 teaspoon vanilla

½ cup buttermilk

2 cups unbleached all-purpose flour

2½ teaspoons baking powder

½ teaspoon salt

½ teaspoon powdered cinnamon

1 cup fresh cranberries, or, when not in season, dried cranberries ("Craisins")

Dissatisfied with Life

Live in the present, it's all there is. Enjoy today to its fullest by being in the moment.

There's something missing, but you don't know what it is. You feel there must be more to life. You know you should be grateful for what you have, but somehow it's not enough.

Fulfillment comes from having a sense of your own worth, integrating your belief systems with the way you live your life, knowing what makes you happy, balancing the responsibilities in your life, and finding your place in the community.

Reach out. Endeavoring to do acts of kindness and generosity on a daily basis will transform the way you live your life. Live according to your values, not those of the magazines and movies.

Help thy neighbor. It's the mortar that binds the world. Be the kind of person you would want to have as a friend. Be honest in all your dealings. Make heartfelt gestures part of your life and you'll find deep satisfaction.

kind

reach

Live out your highest aspirations. Strive to be the best person you can be—not for anyone else, but because it will make you feel good.

What would you like people to say about you when you're gone? Generous, mature, confident…a life filled with harmony and love and laughter. What's preventing it from happening? Only you!

And let's hear a little Life Appreciation—find at least one thing to be grateful for every day. Make it a habit, think about the day's blessings when you brush your teeth at night.

Try This First

Pretend. Act as if you were the person you'd like to be, living the best of all possible lives. You can begin being the person you want to be this minute, right from where you are now. No need to wait until you get richer, thinner, or less stressed. Change your thinking from, "I'll be happy when I lose five pounds," to, "Because I'm happy, I'll be able to lose five pounds." The curious irony is that when you accept yourself just as you are, then you can change.

Be the kind of person you would want to have as a friend. Overlook minor insults and criticisms. Practice small kindnesses—let a car pass, hold open a door without thought of reciprocation. The benefits to you are much more than the benefits to them!

out

good

Full-of-Good-Things Tabbouleh

Happiness and health are connected. To be the best you can be, you must have the best fuel.

For optimal health, your body needs as much variety in food as possible, preferably twenty to twenty-five different foods a day. Taking a daily multivitamin pill won't give you the same disease-fighting power of whole foods. Nobody knows which of the many chemicals in, for example, a tomato does the work of keeping our cells healthy. Scientists still are learning about phytochemicals, a whole new way apart from vitamin, mineral, and fiber content, to evaluate the health-enhancing and disease-fighting power of food.

The best ways to eat a variety of foods is to eat products that combine more than one type of food, for example, bread that contains seeds, grains, and fruit. Salads are a great way to consume a lot of different foods in one day, too. Increase their nutrient content by making them brightly colored: add green, yellow, orange, and red vegetables. A few nuts and seeds add vitamin E and fiber.

This is a sweeter version of the regular tomato tabbouleh. It's good to take to work or on picnics, and it tastes even better when the flavors

Smile, listen, hug, touch.
Show your enthusiasm
and spontaneity.
Share your joy of life.

things

generous

Ingredients

1 cup bulgur

boiling water

1/3 cup chives or scallions

1 cup lightly packed chopped
   parsley (If you have a small
   food processor, haul it out
   now.)

1 cup golden raisins or currants

juice of 2 limes (Don't make do
   with lemons instead, it's not
   the same.)

1/4 cup canola oil

have had a chance to mingle. Bulgur is wheat kernels that have been steamed, dried, and crushed; you can find it in health-food stores. (It's not exactly the same as cracked wheat.)

Preparation

Put bulgur in a bowl and pour over enough boiling water to cover it. Cover the bowl and put aside for at least 30 minutes—until the water is all absorbed.

Add remaining ingredients, toss well. Refrigerate for at least an hour.

Serving Suggestion

Tabbouleh is good with a roast chicken (buy one at the local deli or supermarket if roasting one yourself seems too ambitious), and it makes a great picnic food. Take your lunch outdoors and appreciate nature. Or eat late, under the stars. Spread a blanket in your backyard and look for fireflies. Or, for serious star-gazing and meteor showers, find a place where artificial lights don't obscure the stars. Consider infinity.

Crème de la Corn Bread

Corn is a good food for steadying blood sugar levels. It has B vitamins and vitamin C, potassium and magnesium to ward off fatigue.

Two different kinds of corn in this recipe make for a delicious corn bread.

Cherish the things and people that make you effective.

Attempt to be the best you can be.

Ingredients

1 cup whole-wheat pastry flour

⅓ cup cornmeal (You can use either a fine or coarse grind, although the coarse, whole-grain, stone-ground, or water-milled cornmeal is more nutritious.)

⅓ cup sugar

3 teaspoons baking powder

¾ teaspoon salt

½ cup skim milk

1 egg, lightly beaten

2 tablespoons canola oil

1 8½-ounce can cream-style corn

1 15-ounce can whole kernel corn niblets, drained

Preparation

Preheat the oven to 425° F. Lightly coat an 8-inch square baking dish with nonstick spray. Or, for a crisp, dark crust, bake this the traditional way in a heavy, cast-iron skillet. Grease it well and let it heat up inside the preheated oven while you make the batter. The batter will sizzle as it's poured in the pan.

In a large bowl, combine the flour, cornmeal, sugar, baking powder, and salt.

In a small bowl, combine the milk, egg, oil, and cream-style corn. Pour over the flour mixture. Mix until the dry ingredients are moistened, don't overmix. Fold in the corn niblets.

Pour into the prepared baking dish or skillet. Bake for 20 minutes, or until a toothpick inserted into the center of the bread comes out clean.

Cool on a wire rack. Cut into squares.

Serving Suggestion

Have a small bunch of red grapes with the cornbread. Or go for a whole delicious Southern meal of baked beans, barbecued chicken, collards, and black-eyed peas.

> "Cooking is like love.
> It should be entered
> into with abandon or
> not at all."
>
> —Harriet Van Horne

Lovesick

Hold a man responsible for how he treats you, not for how you feel about yourself.

A successful marriage—or relationship—is not luck, it's an achievement. You have to work at it. But then, you have to work for anything worth having. The work can be difficult, because true intimacy means being so open with another that we become very vulnerable to hurt.

If you are suffering from a broken heart, it may be some comfort to know that every woman who's ever lived has felt the sting of unrequited love, or the ache of a relationship that's unravelled, and has survived. You will, too. One day, you will be able to spend whole hours at a time without thinking of him. Meanwhile, use this time to assess what you gained from the relationship—even if it wasn't a proper relationship. Did you see qualities in him that you definitely want (or don't want) in your next boyfriend? Did you learn something about yourself?

You have your own homework to do before you decide to join your life with another. What are your preconceptions, hopes, and fears about marriage, and what are they based on? How far have you evolved as a person? Are you attracted to him for traits you wish you had yourself? People who have repressed part of their own

personalities often look for those qualities in others. Be forewarned: what you love about him you may come to hate about him. On the other hand, turn his flaws around and you'll find his virtues. (For example, he's a cheapskate—but we've never been in debt.)

A woman never should commit herself, in the first place, to a man she doesn't trust and can't respect. If you're dating, ask yourself, who in my family does this person resemble? How does that make me feel? And is that good or bad? What kind of person does he need me to be? Is that who I really am?

A good relationship happens when both people are committed to being close to each other, and want to use the closeness to find out more about themselves. Both are constantly evolving as individuals and as a couple.

There's an old Italian proverb that translates, more or less, to, "Listen to what he says, but watch his feet." The things a man actually does reveal his true self far more than his words do.

Now, while you're missing him, is the time to watch your own feet—what do your own actions reveal about yourself? Whether he's gone for good or just on hiatus, you're going to have to learn to stand firmly on your own two feet to get through life. Lean on the structure of ritual to get you through—revise the ones you and he used to do together, and create new ones for yourself.

Try This First

Today, make yourself feel cherished, important, and respected. If you are in a relationship, resurrect the shared enthusiasms that brought you together. And when was the last time you paid him a sincere compliment? Do it now. If you are missing him, think back and resurrect an activity you loved to do before you met him, one that you never did together.

The secret to getting him to change: reward him every time he gets it right.

Stop wishing he were different. If he's basically a fine person, ride out the low points.

If he's the most important person in my life, am I treating him as if he is? If he's not, why aren't I with someone who is?

Jam Session Apricot Bread

Dried apricots are a good source of vitamin A, iron, and magnesium, which is needed for a healthy nervous system.

This is not only rich and moist and low-fat, but it's the quickest quick bread you'll ever come across because the blender or food processor does all the work for you in seconds.

Only people with a solid sense of self are mature enough to merge their life with someone else and not fear losing themselves.

Ingredients

1¼ cups all-purpose flour

3½ teaspoon baking powder

½ teaspoon salt

¼ teaspoon each ground ginger, nutmeg, allspice, and cinnamon

1 12-ounce jar of apricot jam

1 6-ounce jar of baby food apricots

1 teaspoon vanilla

3 tablespoons canola oil

2 cups dried apricots

2 eggs

Preparation

Preheat oven to 350° F and grease a 8x4x3-inch loaf pan.

In a large bowl sift flour, baking powder, salt, and spices.

Put the apricot jam, baby food apricots, vanilla, oil, dried apricots, and eggs into a food processor or blender, process just until the apricots have been chopped up. (The mixture will be lumpy, but that's OK.)

Add the ingredients you just processed to the flour mixture, stirring until just combined.

Bake at 350°F for 50 minutes or an hour. (This is a moist bread, so a knife inserted near the center may not come out clean when it's done, but it will brown and spring back when touched lightly in the center.)

Serving Suggestion

If you are suffering through that stage of heartbreak when nothing but ice cream will ease the pain, make some apricot bread to eat with it. The sweetness will make you feel better. Unbelievable as it may seem now, you will survive and you will be a stronger person. Nobody dies of a broken heart. It isn't that easy.

cherish

Charming Chicken Salad

Scientists have found one food that may have an aphrodisiac effect—celery! Celery contains androsterone (a hormone released through perspiration), which is supposed to be irresistible.

Take the skin off the chicken, even though it's delicious, to cut the fat calories. And if you don't have mangoes, use peaches.

Preparation

Take the meat off the chicken in good, big chunks.

Mix the dressing of yogurt, mayonnaise, chutney, and lime juice.

Toss chicken, celery, and mango in the dressing.

Serving Suggestion

Serve him chicken salad with garlic bread and watch how he eats. What flavors turn him on? Does he save the best bits for last? Chew with his mouth open? It can be a better indication of what kind of person he is than anything else! Does he eat with passion and enjoyment? If you find his messy plate endearing, you're in love. If not, the honeymoon's over.

Ingredients

1 roast chicken already cooked (about 2 pounds)

¼ cup plain nonfat yogurt

¼ cup light mayonnaise

¼ cup mango chutney (Available in most supermarkets, in the condiment section near ketchup. Use the leftovers on grilled meats, with curries or as a dipping sauce.)

juice from one lime

3 celery stalks, chopped

2 mangoes or 2 peaches, peeled, pitted, and chopped

Forgive and forget. It's essential.

> "Ah, self-pity. The only kind that really counts."
>
> —Oscar Levant

Jealous

Never feel rich enough, pretty enough, smart enough, or thin enough? Take yourself out of the Comparathon. Envy is an emotion that really depletes your energy—you can become so busy weighing other people's success and failures that you won't be living your own life. Seek, instead, to become your true self.

Someone who is jealous is concentrating on getting and having and not sharing, and does not have rewarding relationships with others.

We live in a society that over-emphasizes the importance of physical appearance. As children, we learn to assess our worth by weighing the amount of attention we receive in relation to our peers. But feeling compelled to prove yourself by comparison and competition condemns you to fight an endless, lonely battle. It's tiring to have to keep creating a perfect self to display to others. A life based on sharing pleasure is much more enjoyable.

Instead of seeking out proof that others have more of everything than you do, concentrate on building your sense of self-worth.

Try This First

Do you realize that when that "wish-I-were-like-her" feeling strikes strongly, you are being shown what's really important to you? Make use of this emotion to set goals for yourself right now. If you are sure something someone else has—a law degree, a diamond ring, a child—will improve your life, start planning to acquire one of your own. If jealousy is driving you, at least make sure it's in the right direction.

seek

Thought to Chew on in the Kitchen

Do I really believe that my worth can be measured by the amount of love and attention I get from someone else, or the material possessions I have? How can I bolster my self-esteem?

Upside-Down Green Apple of My Eye Cake

As James Baldwin wrote, "No kitchen is as sunny as the kitchen of our childhood."

The warm-kitchen smells from childhood can bring back vivid memories of a time when you had everything you needed. Cinnamon and apple smells are the most powerful.

There is no need to frost this cake.

If your springform pan is elderly, it's probably not watertight. Either wrap foil around the bottom or put an old cookie tray on the rack beneath it in the oven (you know you'll be annoyed if you have to wipe up those baked-on drips).

Take the high road. It will make your life more peaceful. Let someone else grab the only cab, squeeze in before you at the supermarket or have the last slice of cake. Bask in your generosity.

If all your energy is taken up with hating yourself for being envious, you'll never be free to make positive life changes.

Preparation

Put the apples in a microwave-safe bowl, sprinkle over the brown sugar, cook uncovered on high for five minutes, stir, then cook another 5 minutes.

Heat oven to 350° F. Grease an 8-inch springform pan.

Pour off the juice from the cooked apples—otherwise the cake will be so moist you'll have to call it Apple Soup. I know it's a waste, but you could always add some regular apple juice to it and drink the result.

Sift together flour, baking soda, salt, baking powder, cinnamon, and cloves into a clean bowl.

Beat sugar and egg with an electric beater in another clean bowl until thoroughly blended.

Add oil and mix well. Add vanilla, applesauce, and apple butter and stir.

Mix the dry ingredients into the wet just until they're combined, no more.

Take about a cup of the batter and mix with the apples. (If you don't do this, the apples will fall off the top of the cake like mosaic tiles not properly set.) Pour the apple mixture into your greased pan, then pour the rest of the batter on top.

Bake 30 to 40 minutes, until a knife inserted in the center of the cake comes out clean. Let it sit in the oven until cool. Turn it upside down and be careful as you take the top off.

Serving Suggestion

Serve to your rival, with humility. Diffuse the competition by reaching out. Issue an invitation for coffee and cake. Resolve to enjoy the qualities that make him or her so desirable, instead of wishing they belonged to you. In the end, you may find you're perfectly content to be who you are.

look on the

Ingredients

4 small or 3 large apples, peeled, cored, and chopped into chunks. A mixture of different types of apples works best. Use Golden Delicious, Granny Smith, Rome, or any type of apple suitable for pies.

½ cup brown sugar

1 cup flour

1 teaspoon baking soda

¼ teaspoon salt

½ teaspoon baking powder

¼ teaspoon cinnamon

¼ teaspoon cloves

⅓ cup sugar

1 large egg

4 tablespoons canola oil

1 teaspoon vanilla

3 generous tablespoons chunky applesauce

3 generous tablespoons apple butter

Is fire superior to air? In nature, everything just is.

Mean Green Gazpacho

Chives are really easy to grow in a pot on a window ledge, and will provide you with instant, fresh, onion-flavored stalks to add to all sorts of dishes. Members of the onion family contain protective HDL cholesterol, which help offset the effects of a high-fat diet.

You can make this gazpacho a day ahead of time, so the flavors have a chance to develop, then strain it for a more elegant appearance before serving.

Preparation

Process everything together in the blender. Serve cold on a hot day.

Serving Suggestion

Drink this from a glass for a quick, cooling-off drink by itself, or serve with a Quick Bean Burrito Wrap.

Ingredients

1 large cucumber, peeled and cut into chunks

1 large green bell pepper, seeded and chopped

1 stalk of celery chopped into chunks

juice from half a lime

1 cup white grape juice

1 teaspoon chopped onion or chives

2 teaspoons apple cider vinegar

1 tablespoon fat-free sour cream

There is justice: the girl with the skin you'd love to have will get wrinkles. You'll look back at the guy who seems so desirable now and laugh. Time heals.

There's a reason runners don't look back. If you concentrate on someone else's performance, your own will suffer.

Mean Green Coleslaw

Raw green cabbage is a good source of folic acid, protective antioxidants, and glucosinolates which contain substances with anti-cancer properties.

Preparation

Put the coleslaw mix into a salad bowl. Peel the apples, then grate over the cabbage through a coarse grater.

Mix up the dressing ingredients and pour over the whole thing.

Serving Suggestion

Coleslaw goes well with a selection of cold meats from the deli for a fast meal. But serve the meal nicely. Treat yourself as you would a welcome guest. Don't wait for others to validate you.

Ingredients

1 package pre-chopped coleslaw cabbage mix from the super-market

2 apples (Granny Smith, Fuji, or Red Delicious)

Dressing:

½ cup fat-free mayonnaise

½ cup nonfat sour cream

¼ cup white grape juice or apple juice

salt and pepper to taste

peace

of mind

"She got even in a way that was almost cruel. She forgave them."

—Ralph McGill on Eleanor Roosevelt

Vengeful

Resentment stifles your energy and happiness. Shed the burden of carrying a grudge and you will feel lighter. If you are still angry about things that happened to you years ago, you are wasting your life in being angry at people. It'll cripple you.

Forgiveness takes time because it must be genuine, not forced. Try to uncover the motivation behind your enemy's actions, try to see beyond the deed itself.

Often, letting go of resentment involves grieving for yourself and the mistakes you made.

If you can write it all out, and continue to write about how you feel every day, you will gradually see your hatred diminish. Record exactly how you feel, every bit of sadness and anger. No matter the form of the writing—a journal entry, a letter, etc.—the important thing is to rid yourself of the poison, not to keep up a feud with an enemy.

Forgiving someone does not mean taking on the role of victim. If you are taking legal steps for justice, you will be more focussed if you are not blinded by anger. And remember that the things you put your

When you obsess about your enemies you're letting them live in your head rent-free.

patience

energy into are what you end up getting in life. Your best chance of a happy life is in forgiving. Forgiving lets you let go of the hate and get on with your life.

Is there any truth to the saying that revenge is a dish best eaten cold? Are cold foods good for you? They may help you lose weight. Your body has to work a little bit harder to warm up cold foods to body temperature. Depending on how cold it is, you'll burn fifteen to twenty-five calories for each glass of cold water you drink. Not much, but it could add up.

Try This First

The first step is to stop obsessing about the wrong that was done. You must make peace of mind your only goal right now. Even if you feel you can never forgive, at least let go.

Convert all that energy that you put into being angry into bringing about good changes in your life.

As Helen Gurley Brown says, "The blueprint for your revenge is built into their DNA." In other words, people who treat you badly treat others badly, too and therefore find themselves in trouble eventually.

Thought to Chew on in the Kitchen

How can I put the hours I'm spending plotting revenge to good use? Is there a book here somewhere? Jot down notes for the perfect murder story, or write that How-To-Get-Boyfriend-Revenge Manual.

Peas-Offering Soup

Peas have potassium, iron, and vitamin A. Frozen peas may actually be a better source of vitamin C than fresh ones. Thaw frozen foods just enough to cook them properly—bacteria multiplies during thawing.

This soup is a beautiful fresh green in color and has a clean, fresh taste.

Preparation

Process everything (except the optional garnish) in the blender, adding some water if it won't start blending. Pour the soup into bowls and crumble a little feta cheese on top if you have it. Serve immediately.

Serving Suggestion

Serve this soup to begin a meal on a summer evening. Follow with a lamb dish.

It's the oldest, most symbolic peace gesture there is: sitting down to a meal with your opponent, if you can bring yourself to do it. If not, turn the revenge energy into a positive force by making this meal for someone who always does right by you.

Ingredients

16-ounce bag of frozen green peas, thawed enough so it isn't a solid block

1 cup chicken broth

1 cup buttermilk or low-fat yogurt

2 or 3 mint leaves (If you don't have any mint, make the soup anyway and leave it out.)

1 tablespoon chives

extra water if necessary

optional garnish: feta cheese

focus

see

Reconciliation Cold Sesame Noodles

Peanut butter boosts levels of choline in the brain which slows age-related memory loss.

Many sesame noodle recipes list obscure ingredients that mean a special trip to an Oriental grocery before you can start to put them together. This one calls for things you most likely have on hand—and gives you choices, too.

A lifetime of looking back in anger is no way to live.

When you forgive, you set yourself free.

beyond

Ingredients

happiness

1 pound of egg noodles, or Japanese buckwheat noodles (soba)

½ cup peanut butter (If you have it, use chunky peanut butter, the "natural" type that separates out, but any sort will do.)

1 tablespoon soy sauce

3 tablespoons sesame or canola oil

3 tablespoons chicken broth (or dissolve a cube in boiling water)

¼ cup dry sherry

2 tablespoons apricot preserves *or* apricot nectar *or* prune juice *or* mango chutney

½ inch fresh ginger, grated

Optional extras: about a half cup cooked, diced chicken

2 tablespoons roasted peanuts

½ cucumber, peeled, seeded, and cut into strips

2 tablespoons chopped scallions or chives

1 tablespoon toasted sesame seeds

½ cup steamed, diced snow peas or water chestnuts

Preparation

Cook the egg noodles or soba according to package directions. Drain well and cool.

While the noodles are cooking, mix together in a large bowl the peanut butter, soy sauce, canola or sesame oil, chicken broth, sherry, apricot preserves, and fresh ginger.

Taste. Make it thinner or add more of an ingredient. Vary the contents until it tastes good to you. When the noodles are cool, add them to the sauce. Then add any of the optional ingredients that you may have on hand.

Serving Suggestion

Follow cold sesame noodles with fortune cookies and green tea ice cream for dessert.

"As to marriage or celibacy, let a man take which course he will—he will be sure to repent it."

—Socrates

Lonely

You're not dateless, you're date-free. Splitting up with your boyfriend means you have more time for your other friends. It's all in how you look at things, how you reframe your life.

Think of all the selfish, silly, indulgent things you can do when there's no one to raise an eyebrow—you can have a party on the spur of the moment, eat mangoes over the kitchen sink, or conduct whole orchestras in your pajamas. You're liberated!

There's absolutely no reason you can't do whatever you want to do right now. You don't have to wait until you're married to start thinking about buying an apartment. You don't have to wait for a honeymoon to travel to exciting places.

If you're alone now, this is a chance to get to know yourself and become your own best friend. Discover what you like about yourself, otherwise your own company will become unbearable.

Living alone forces you to come to terms with your truest self—and people who are attuned to themselves are able to read other people quickly and clearly.

Watching the sunset and wish someone was with you? But you'd miss the wonder of it as you gazed up at him, watching for his response! Instead, be totally in the moment.

Give yourself a massage. Yes, you can. Instead of feeling sorry for yourself, place your hand on the opposite shoulder and knead your own neck and shoulder muscles.

But if you are yearning to connect, take a class—any class. You'll find yourself in a room full of like-minded people attempting something new, so you all immediately have something in common and lots to talk about.

Talk to interesting-looking strangers. Walk a dog in the park on the weekend. Enlarge your circle of acquaintances. Concentrate on giving and sharing—start an investment group, offer to babysit, attend a meeting. Give out an aura of neediness, and no one will want anything to do with you. Get involved in projects, and other people will gather to see what's going on.

And, if you're looking for a lover, search for a friend.

Try This First

You truly have to understand who you are before you can connect meaningfully with other people. Wanting to get married because you can't bear living alone is a terrible basis for a relationship. Learn how to be totally happy by yourself, and you will attract the sort of people you want to be around.

Relating to others means really listening to them with all your senses.

If you're seeking things from someone else that you need to find within yourself, you're always going to feel lonely and alienated.

How have you handled solitude so far in your life? Constructively or destructively?

85

Do I feel threatened by
intimacy with others? Even
though I feel lonely, am I
choosing isolation as easier to
bear?

Share-Me Peanut Butter Cookies

These two quick cookie recipes have nothing to do with nutrition. They're just sweet treats to whip up quickly—you can get everything you need at the corner convenience store.

Preparation

Heat oven to 350° F.

Beat egg well, mix in peanut butter and sugar. Add nuts.

Drop in rounded spoonfuls two inches apart on a greased cookie sheet. Bake 10 to 12 minutes, or until the bottoms of the cookies are slightly browned.

Makes nine cookies.

Serving Suggestion

When you're lonely, eating can become a way to fill an emotional void. These are for sharing, don't eat them all yourself! While the cookies are baking, telephone someone and arrange a visit. Foods shared bond the giver and the taker.

Ingredients

8 ounces of smooth peanut butter (about 1 cup)

1 large egg

1 tablespoon sugar

2½ ounces of honey-roasted peanuts, crushed

Friendly Coconut Macaroons

Preparation

Heat oven to 350° F.

Mix flour and coconut well, then add enough sweetened condensed milk to make a thick batter.

Use a tablespoon to scoop up a small ball of batter, use another to scrape it off onto the greased cookie sheet.

Bake exactly 20 minutes. Cookies should be pale straw-colored, not brown. Cool on the cookie sheet before removing.

Makes 18 cookies.

Serving Suggestion

Have a few of these cookies after a meal of spaghetti. As Christopher Morley once said, "No one is lonely while eating spaghetti, it requires too much attention."

Ingredients

⅓ cup all-purpose flour

2½ cups shredded coconut (one 7-ounce packet)

⅔ cup (about half a 14-ounce can) fat-free sweetened condensed milk (Yes, they do make fat-free sweetened condensed milk, but in some areas it may be difficult to find, in which case you can use the regular variety.)

come to *terms*

Fighting with Family

One of the most important psychological tasks we face as adults is to come to terms with our parents and our feelings toward them.

If you completely renounce your parents, it's like cutting off a piece of yourself. You must make peace with them (even if they're no longer around) to be at peace.

To understand why your parents did some of the things they did, explore their lives as young people—the geographic location and the social context of their era. As a child, you often assume your parents are behaving in a certain way because of something you've done—now you can better understand the pressures they were under.

Acknowledge the good things you've been blessed with by being born to these people—a love of music, a feisty spirit. And take time to talk to your grandparents, aunts, uncles. You will discover more about yourself than you anticipate.

It's not until you do your homework about your past that you can learn how to live your own life. When you stop blaming your parents for your limitations, you will finally be free.

You can't change your parents' behavior, but you can change your reaction to it. It's not easy. The convenience and familiarity of being angry at your parents can be hard to give up.

Try This First

Think of what you'd like to get from your relationship with your parents today. Aim for a relationship based on the way all of you are *now*. If your parents are no longer alive, you can still talk to them, in your own mind, and resolve your differences.

When we were children, our lives depended on pleasing our parents to get what we needed. The ways we found to please them are the ways we interact today with the rest of the world.

Most of us never let our parents grow up, so that we don't have to grow up ourselves.

Thought to Chew on in the Kitchen

How can I be to myself the kind of mother or father I wish I'd had? How can I give myself the love and nurturing I crave?

Rice Pudding for Your Inner Five-Year-Old

Remember licking the bowl the cake was mixed in, milk mustaches, and catching the drip from the ice cream cone with your tongue?

Watch a baby get totally involved with puréed vegetables to recapture some of that feeling, and understand your attitude toward food now. Eat some rice pudding and explore your childhood memories.

This recipe uses raw rice. You make it in the microwave, which means that although it takes 40 minutes, that's all doing-something-else time, not standing-over-a-hot-stove-stirring time.

No one can change what happened to you as a child, but you make your own choices now. You're in control of your own life. Yes, you are what your parents made you—but if you stay that way, it's your own fault.

Preparation

Stir together the rice, salt, sugar, water, and raisins if you're using them. Select a very large microwave-safe bowl (if it's small, the milk may boil over).

Microwave for 10 minutes on *high*.

Remove the bowl from the microwave, stir, add the skim milk and return to microwave and cook on *high* again, for 10 minutes.

recapture
peace

Again, remove, stir, add the evaporated milk and microwave on *high*, for 10 minutes more.

Okay, now taste a few grains of rice, but be careful, they're hot!

If the rice is done, you're just cooking it now to reach a desired consistency—probably five or six minutes more, again on *high*.

Stir in the vanilla. Let stand 10 minutes.

Sprinkle with nutmeg before serving.

Serving Suggestion

Warm rice pudding—just a little, by itself—is an ideal comforting snack before bed on a cold night.

For most of us, the links between food, reward, consequences, and punishment get confused when we're young. Did your parents say things like, "If you're good, you can have an ice cream," or, "One more spoonful, that's a good girl"? Think about the messages you absorbed about food.

It's OK to reward yourself with food as a special treat, as long as you're aware of what you're doing, and the habit doesn't become uncontrollable.

Ingredients

½ cup uncooked Arborio short-grain rice (This is the type that's perfect for risotto, for creamiest results. Don't use parboiled or quick-cooking rice.)

⅛ teaspoon salt

¼ cup sugar

I cup water

I cup skim milk

I cup fat-free evaporated milk

I teaspoon vanilla extract

½ cup raisins (entirely optional—some people have strong opinions about raisins in rice pudding)

nutmeg (again, only if you like it)

Whatever happened in your childhood, you survived it.

(relatively) *easy*

Relatively Easy Chicken Broth

Studies show that chicken soup actually does alleviate cold symptoms more effectively than acetaminophen by soothing sore throats and clearing congestion. Mother knows best!

Use this as a base for chicken soup, or enjoy as it is—a clear chicken stock.

The best soup is made with chicken backs, but if you can't get them, use just the legs. If you use a whole chicken, you get into the messy business of trying to salvage the meat—it's much easier to just buy the parts you want and throw all the solids away later. (Although, if you often cook whole chickens, you can collect the backs in a plastic bag in the freezer—but don't mix cooked meat with raw meat.)

There's no "right" amount of vegetables to use when making chicken stock, use whatever you have on hand, but use no more than a cup of each vegetable or the chicken flavor will be overpowered.

Serving Suggestion

Serve this soup to the chicken soup maven in your family, or the friend who knows all about the healing power of food. ("Eat, eat, you'll feel better!") Compare notes. Ask her secrets. Write down her recipes. This is what families are for.

Seek out your oldest living relative and ask her about remedies like honey and lemon juice for coughs, mustard plasters for chests, and cloves for toothaches. These are ways women have healed their families for generations.

Ingredients

1 small onion, peeled, and chopped

2 tablespoons canola oil

2 or 3 pounds chicken backs cut up (It's important to cut up the chicken into small pieces—there's a lot of goodness inside the bones. If you're using legs, hack into 3 pieces.)

8 to 12 cups cold water

1 carrot, scraped, and chopped

leftover leafy tops of celery (no more than one cup)

leftover turnip or parsnip parts (no more than one cup)

a few sprigs of parsley (no more than one cup)

Preparation

Sauté the onion in the oil, add the chicken pieces, and cook until they start to brown. Cover and simmer chicken in its own juices for 20 minutes.

Add the cold water. (When you want to get flavor out, use cold water. When you want to keep flavor in meat, boiling water seals it in.) Add the carrot, celery, and turnip or parsnip pieces.

Heat the water and allow to boil rapidly for 15 minutes, then reduce to barely a simmer and let cook for at least 2 hours. (The longer the cooking, the richer the soup.) Add more water if necessary.

Strain the soup and throw away all the solids. Let it cool, then refrigerate overnight.

Remove congealed fat from the top. Use paper towels to blot up any remaining fat. You can freeze this broth for later use.

understanding

Feeling Alienated

When other people hurt you, don't react by trying to protect yourself from life. Strengthen yourself so you can let more life in.

Human beings need the emotional sustenance of family and friends to know unconditional love and support. It's necessary for our health. Create your own "family" by spending more time with kindred spirits—those people who make you feel happy, alive, and comfortable.

Female bonding is cheaper than therapy and much more fun. Women are so good at supporting and inspiring others—their men, their children, and especially each other. It's one of the things we do best.

Spend time on a regular basis with women who have similar lives and problems—you'll feel less isolated and pressured. You don't have to struggle alone. Why not start your own support group? Gather several friends together every week. Give each other a turn to talk—to vent, to ask for help, to tell the group about your week.

You also need to appreciate the friends you already have. When you're with someone else, be with that person 100 percent. Don't pretend to find her interesting, actually find out something interesting about her.

bond

compliments

Give friends compliments of the *you* type—not, "I like your blue blouse," but, "You always wear the most wonderful colors!"

Stay away from those who tend to extract the joy out of everything. There are two kinds of people to avoid at all costs: chronic complainers and those who criticize your dreams and aspirations. When someone is hostile, don't react to her anger, don't escalate the conflict. Be aware that she is, right now, at the mercy of her emotions. You should endeavor to be calm, polite, and in control.

If you lack close, caring relationships, you need to develop feelings of empathy with anyone and everyone! Commiserate with others waiting in line, ask the doorman how his day's going. Take the risk and smile at someone. Connect.

Try This First

First, you have to be friends with yourself. If you don't love yourself, other people pick up the sense of dissatisfaction.

Moods are contagious: be around happy people. Let them infect you with their happiness, don't bring them down.

Amiable Avocado Soup

Each avocado has about 275 calories and 25 grams of fat each, but only five of the fat grams are the unhealthy, saturated kind, the rest are heart-healthy. Avocados also have an antioxidant that helps fight heart disease and cancer, plus folate, which has been found to alleviate depression. And avocados contain magnesium, which has a calming effect on the nervous system.

Treasure those people with whom you can most easily be yourself. Your friends give you life because they help you discover yourself.

smile

1 cup chicken broth

1 boiling potato, peeled and
  quartered

1 ripe avocado, peeled, pitted,
  cubed

2 cups lowfat buttermilk

1 cup nonfat yogurt

appreciate

Preparation

Put the potato and broth in a saucepan. (The potato should be covered with liquid, so add water to the broth if there's not enough.)

Simmer until the potato can be pierced easily with a fork. Turn the heat off and let cool.

Put the potato and broth in the blender with all the other ingredients and process until smooth.

Cool in the refrigerator for 30 minutes. A swirl of yogurt on top of each serving looks classy.

Serving Suggestion

Since people always love to congregate in the kitchen, serve meals there, especially if you have a large, open kitchen. It communicates a cozy, informal ease. Keep avocado soup in the refrigerator to serve with pita bread and salads when people drop by. Open a new bottle of wine. Celebrate. When you are with people, you are with life.

The best friends know when to talk, when to listen, and when to bring cookies.

Company's Coming Lamb Chops

Lack of iron can make you feel tired and overwhelmed. Women, especially if they eat fewer than 2,500 calories a day, need to make sure they're getting enough lean meat. Occasional small red-meat, high-fat indulgences keep you from feeling deprived.

Foil packets—the same method that works so well with fish—also cook lamb chops perfectly. You can wrap them up before your guests arrive, so they'll be all ready to put in the oven.

You need people who respect and appreciate you—and you need to respect and appreciate your friends.

together

Ingredients

For each person you'll need:

1 good-quality loin or baby lamb chop

1 slice of eggplant

1 slice of onion

1 slice of green pepper

1 slice of tomato

1 tablespoon of sherry

1 10-inch square of heavy-duty aluminum foil

connect

Preparation

Place a chop on a square of foil and pile the slices of eggplant, onion, pepper, and tomato on top. Fold up the edges of the foil, pour on the sherry, and make neat little packets of each chop.

Put them all in a baking dish or pie plate and bake for an hour at 350° F.

Serving Suggestion

Lamb chops and a microwaved sweet potato make an easy meal. Eat with family and friends often. Meals eaten with others supply more than just nutrition: children learn healthy eating habits; social networks are built through sharing cultural, ethnic, and family customs; and we all thrive when we connect with others.

"Ask your child
what he wants for
dinner only if he's
buying."

—Fran Lebowitz

Working Mother Guilt

Parenting can be the cause of the worst guilt feelings you'll ever have—but running yourself ragged trying to be the perfect mom is counterproductive. Stress is contagious.

Instead, demonstrate to the kids how to live a busy—but happy—life. Forget the dishes, read to them instead. Your children will remember being part of a happy household where everyone is involved, they won't remember the time the ironing didn't get done. Give up rigid definitions—of dinner, sleep, everything. Lower your standards.

Your guilt may be masking your own feelings of loss and need. You need to concentrate on the kids. The fact that you missed baby's first steps isn't important. He will be happy showing you how he can stand up over and over again. The fact that you weren't there the first time doesn't bother him—it only bothers you. Just enjoy the times you are there.

When in doubt, find out what matters to the people you feel guilty about neglecting. Ask the kids which they really want you to attend, their music recital or Little League practice. Before you hire help,

Do the best you can and then let go. The letting go is important. Your kids need you to be relaxed and happy, not stressed.

Consider whether you are being manipulated into guilt by people who want to feel better about themselves.

care

think about the best ways to use that help. You could hire a babysitter to watch the kids while you get groceries, or you could hire a teenager to do the shopping while you play with the kids, instead.

What children really need is self-esteem, trusting relationships, and parents who have realistic expectations of them.

Think about how your mother and father brought you up. Decide not only what you think they did right and wrong, but also whether that style is right for your kids. Define for yourself your role as mother. You need to decide on your own values and do what you can to meet them. Give up worrying about the rest.

Guilt is an emotion you can just decide to give up, cold turkey.

Try This First

Care for yourself—your own happiness and well-being must be in place before you can share it with others. Would you allow your kids to eat what you ate today? Would you allow them to feel as bad as you do and not help?

It's not whether you go out to work or stay at home—it's how you feel about it. Stay-at-home moms can be just as stressed as working mothers.

Guilt is the most useless emotion there is. Often, things happen without anyone being at fault.

for yourself

Thought to Chew on in the Kitchen

What good does guilt do? After it has prompted you to assess if you've done all you can for someone, it does no good at all.

Watermelon Whirl

Getting all the seeds out of a watermelon doesn't have to be a hassle. As you're cutting it up, keep aside the seed-dense chunks. Let the kids take them out to the garden to compete in how far they can spit them.

Then, serve them this wonderful frothy pink summertime drink. This recipe makes a batch of drinks for 2 or 3 people.

Preparation

Process together in the blender.

Serving Suggestion

Watermelon whirl goes well with cake at children's birthday parties.

Have you inherited the belief that if you aren't a good cook you aren't a good mother? Today that's an out-moded mindset. It's more important to give your kids healthy food as often as possible.

Ingredients

3 or 4 cups of watermelon, in chunks

1 8-ounce container of "fruit-on-the-bottom"-type low-fat raspberry yogurt

Guilt-Free Chocolate Cake

enjoy

Put some chocolate sauce in a squeeze bottle and write a loving message to the kids around the edge of their plate. If you are someone for whom each bite of chocolate is a little bit of sin, don't pass this attitude on to your kids. It's healthier believing there are no "bad" or "good" foods.

This cake is low-fat—it uses cocoa instead of chocolate—and the kids could help you make it.

Preparation

Preheat oven to 350° F.

Sift together ⅔ cup cocoa, flour, baking powder, and salt.

In another bowl, beat the sugar, oil, egg whites, vanilla, and one cup of water with an electric mixer. Add the flour mixture and stir until batter is smooth. Pour into a nonstick 8-inch round cake pan.

Bake in 350° F oven for 35 to 40 minutes, or until cake begins to pull away from the side of the pan and springs back when lightly touched in the center.

Ingredients

¼ cup canola oil

⅔ cup good quality unsweetened cocoa powder (not the kind of chocolate-milk powder you use for making drinks)

1¼ cups all-purpose flour

1 teaspoon baking powder

¼ teaspoon salt

1¼ cups sugar

2 large egg whites

1 teaspoon vanilla

1 cup cold water

letting go

Serving Suggestion

Instead of frosting, find a lacy paper doily and place it on top of the cake. Sift some confectioners' sugar on top, then gently lift away the doily. Serve with milk.

Easy Cheesy Macaroni & Cheese

Studies show that eating cheeses along with sugary foods counteracts the cavity-causing effects on teeth—the calcium and phosphates form a protective barrier against plaque.

This is an easy version of macaroni and cheese, best made in a shallow dish for lots of crunchy topping.

Serving Suggestion

Show the kids how to play with healthy food. Serve macaroni and cheese with sliced vegetables that have been cut into shapes with little cookie cutters. For dessert, let them make "face" fruit salads: a peach half for the face, grated carrot for the hair, raisins for the eyes, and a strawberry half for the mouth.

Preparation

Place the onion, mustard, and evaporated milk in a blender or food processor. Process for a minute to painlessly chop the onion very fine and combine it with the milk.

Heat the milk mixture in a large, nonstick saucepan, add the cheeses and stir until they've melted.

Combine this sauce with the pasta, and pour it all into a baking dish about 10x6 and 2 inches deep.

Sprinkle the breadcrumbs and extra sharp grated cheddar over the top.

Cook for 30 minutes, or until the top starts to brown, in a 350° F oven.

Ingredients

½ pound cooked elbow, rotelli, fusili, or rotini macaroni—any shape with lots of hiding places for the sauce (Cook until almost but not quite tender, firm to the bite, not over-cooked.)

I small onion, peeled and roughly cut up

¾ cup evaporated skim milk

I teaspoon dry mustard

4 ounces each shredded Cheddar and Monterey Jack cheeses (In some supermarkets, you can buy them already shredded.)

5 ounces shredded Parmesan cheese

Topping:

½ cup sharp Cheddar, shredded

½ cup breadcrumbs

You don't have the power to protect your kids from every hurt, and it's not good for them to grow up believing you do.

objective

Getting Criticized

Every time you are criticized, you have to decide whether it is a valid criticism. Stay objective. Listen carefully to make sure you've understood. Repeat back what you think you've heard.

Say, "Ouch, that hurt!" and ask for clarification.

If you begin to doubt your own competence and self-worth, and start apologizing for everything, consider other people's motives. Sometimes they're giving you advice that would be good for them if they were in your situation, but not for you. Sometimes they are using criticism to keep you under control, humiliate and hurt, or to make themselves feel superior.

Try to ignore a compulsive critic. He does it for the attention, and if you argue, it will reinforce the behavior.

But if you are someone who can never accept criticism gracefully—no matter how constructive—you may, deep inside, doubt your own worth. Sometimes, people who develop a very poor self-image as children form a hard shell of narcissism, and react very strongly when they are criticized.

It may be hard to accept, but on some level you attracted this criticism. If you feel inferior, you attract people who make you feel inferior.

Avoid spending time with people who criticize everyone and everything. It can be catching.

valid

106

If you want to be absolved from all failure, if you insist you are right and project blame on the person who is trying to help, you have work to do on your own self-esteem.

However you respond to criticism, remember that nothing others say can change your own intrinsic worth as a person.

Try This First

Respond to all criticism with, "Interesting opinion, I'll consider it." Then remind yourself of your own worth. When you're ready, decide whether there's a grain of truth in the criticism and what you are going to do about it.

A positive attitude may not end all the criticism, but it will annoy your critics enough to make it worth the effort. Just keep agreeing with chronic criticizers until they get frustrated and give up.

What a dull, uninteresting person you'd have to be for everyone to like you all the time!

Thought to Chew on in the Kitchen

How valid is this criticism? Don't accept it out of habit. Imagine they're talking about someone else. Examine all aspects carefully before you decide to do anything.

Triumphant Truffles

Cocoa butter is high in saturated fat, but it is a fat called stearic acid, which is converted to monounsaturated fat—the not-so-bad kind of fat that olive oil contains, which doesn't raise blood cholesterol levels.

The other good news about chocolate is that it's been found to contain antioxidants called phenols, the same as in red wine, that may help postpone some of the signs of aging. One less thing to feel bad about.

Children who are constantly criticized and whose accomplishments are belittled by their parents often discount their own achievements. If you feel that what you do is not valuable, you may not allow yourself to feel successful.

triumphant

Ingredients

8 ounces semi-sweet chocolate (You must use a good quality chocolate—the finest has 62 to 72 percent cocoa butter. Don't use chocolate chips from the supermarket.)

1 ounce unsalted butter (¼ stick)

1 large egg yolk

1 ounce cognac, Grand Marnier, rum, or Scotch whiskey

unsweetened cocoa to roll the truffles in

Preparation

In a double boiler arrangement, or in a heavy saucepan on top of very low heat, melt the chocolate. It's easy to scorch chocolate, so don't walk away and leave it.

Add the butter. When it's melted, add the egg yolk, and whisk gently for 2 minutes. Add the liqueur, and whisk until smooth.

Put the whole pan in the refrigerator and chill for about two hours or until mixture is firm.

Spread about two tablespoons of cocoa onto a large flat plate.

Take a about a tablespoonful of the chocolate mixture, and, with your fingers straight, hands flat, roll it into a ball.

Then, roll each truffle in the unsweetened cocoa. This recipe should make about 10.

Lick your hands with abandon.

Serving Suggestion

These truffles look very impressive and make a good gift at holiday time (just be sure to tell the lucky recipient to keep them refrigerated). Or serve them yourself after a special meal, with champagne—you'll hear only praise.

Resist the temptation to eat all the chocolate truffles yourself because you don't feel loved. Don't confuse food with love. Find other ways to boost your mood on dark days.

109

Serve baked squash to someone who usually criticizes your cooking—along with something easy like lamb chops—and turn his critical judgment to something benign: ask him to analyze what flavors you've used to make the squash tasty.

Unsquelched Squash

Acorn squashes—the ridged green ones with a splash of yellow that come in the shape of an acorn—are a perfect quick vegetable. They contain fiber, potassium, vitamin C, and beta-carotene.

One acorn squash serves two people. Choose ones that are heavy for their size and blemish-free. They keep for months in a cool, dry place.

Cut the squash in half horizontally and use a spoon to scrape out the seeds.

Trim the bottom of each half so it will stay level. With a fork, prick all over the inside of the squash. Fill the cavity with one of these filling suggestions.

Preparation

Bake in a regular oven for 20 to 30 minutes at 375° F or cover with microwave-safe plastic wrap, one corner loose to let steam escape, and microwave on high for 20 minutes.

Filling Suggestions

1 tablespoon maple syrup and a sprinkle of cinnamon

1 tablespoon orange juice and a sprinkle of light brown sugar, powdered ginger, and chopped walnuts

1 tablespoon applesauce, and a sprinkle of dry sherry, cinnamon

1 tablespoon chutney

1 tablespoon chicken broth

Holiday Blues

The shopping. The wrapping. The regressive sibling rivalry. The calories, the bills, the crowded airports. No wonder you dread this time of year.

We expect so much from the holidays. Maybe it's time to scale back our expectations.

Never count on anyone in your dysfunctional extended family ever changing. Except you: detach and take a new perspective. Watch everyone take on their roles around the dinner table as if you were watching a play. Why did each person take up his or her part? Growing up, what did you learn from each of them?

If the holidays occur deep in the winter months where you live, that in itself may make you feel low. Women are three times more likely to get depressed in dark, cold weather than men are because estrogen and progesterone, the female hormones, are particularly responsive to seasonal changes.

And during the winter months, Seasonal Affective Disorder (SAD) might be making you blue. Lack of sun reduces your levels of serotonin and melatonin, the chemicals that regulate sleep, mood, and

The moment things get hectic, slow down, get organized, and cut back. Decorate a little bit each night. Send online cards. Give everyone the same present—a certificate for a massage or a bottle of wine. You won't lose the holiday spirit, you'll find it.

treats

111

hunger, and that can mean depression, increased appetite, weight gain, and lethargy.

Try to get more protein, and make sure you're getting adequate vitamin D. Try to get outside as much as possible, too, even if it's overcast. Exercise outdoors. Lighten up inside by using high-wattage light bulbs in the lamps that will except them, and by painting your walls a pale color to reflect light. Move your work space near the window. Keep the curtains back and bushes near windows trimmed.

If you are by yourself, this may be an opportunity to get away to somewhere sunny. Or, indulge yourself with special treats that are not connected with the holidays (theaters won't be crowded and traveling is easier). Have one wonderful seasonal symbol—it doesn't have to be a traditional one, that symbolizes the season. A glorious bowl, a special scarf, your favorite holiday food—use it only at this time of the year. Or do something by yourself that has deep meaning for you.

Within your family, decide which activities of the season matter to you. Ask your husband and children which they like best. Talk about your shared holiday memories. Decide which traditions—the ones that make you feel good will toward everyone—to make your own. When choosing your favorites, the only things to consider are simplicity, consistency, and meaning. What worked in the past? Is having a holiday meal that doesn't vary by a single ingredient from year to year essential to your family's sense of tradition? Or maybe the highlight is making ornaments together, or listening to glorious voices singing carols, or creating the annual holiday family photo. Make these activities your rituals, do them wholeheartedly and with gratitude, even if they turn out to be as simple as reading part of a holiday story together.

Don't dismiss the power of ritual. This is the way we renew and reestablish essential human connections to each other.

Try This First

Aim for a pleasant holiday, not a wonderful, memorable, exciting one. Have low expectations and be pleasantly surprised if they're exceeded. Resolve simply to enjoy all the enjoyable things that go along with the holidays.

Who says you have to be superwoman? Set a deadline. After December 20, stop shopping, baking, going to the post office, and all the other chores. Just enjoy.

Thought to Chew on in the Kitchen

What does this time of year mean to me? What would be the ideal way to spend it?

Soothing Purée of Winter Vegetables

You don't have to be intimidated by root vegetables! But you should eat them—vegetables with yellow, orange, and red coloring contain carotenoids, antioxidant plant pigments that are converted to vitamin A by the body and provide all sorts of health benefits, such as reducing the risk of cancer and cataracts.

A healthy diet includes cruciferous vegetables, but if you don't like eating Brussels sprouts, cauliflower, cabbage, or kale, try turnips; they're a cruciferous vegetable, too.

For the following recipe, you don't even have to remember whether the purple ones are turnips or rutabagas or parsnips, as long as you find one of the three.

Puréed vegetables aren't just for babies and invalids—the French have made purées an art form—comfort food that's good for you.

Simply give up doing whichever holiday chore you hate most. Forever.

share

Ingredients

1 carrot

1 potato

1 parsnip or turnip or rutabaga

1 yam or sweet potato

2 cups chicken broth

½ cup fat-free yogurt

½ teaspoon powdered ginger

Preparation

Peel and chop everything into chunks, then boil until soft in the chicken broth.

When cool, process in the blender, in batches if necessary, with the yogurt and ginger.

If you just have one moment of peace and good will to mankind per day, it's enough.

moments

Variation: Roasted Vegetables

The same good winter root vegetables in a more grown-up form.

Preparation

Heat oven to 450° F.

Peel and cut vegetables into chunks. Arrange in a single layer on a baking dish, dribble over the oil, salt, and pepper. Bake 15 minutes, or until tender and browned.

Toss with the concentrate, vinegar, and parsley.

Serving Suggestion

Puréed or roasted, these vegetables are the perfect complement to turkey, at Thanksgiving or any other time. Your local deli or supermarket may even sell roasted turkey breast ready-cooked.

Ingredients

¾ pound carrots

¾ pound parsnips

1½ tablespoons olive oil

salt and pepper

1 tablespoon frozen orange juice concentrate

2 tablespoons balsamic vinegar

2 tablespoons fresh, chopped parsley

Ingredients

1¼ cup sugar

½ cup water

12 ounces cranberries

¾ cup dried apricots, chopped

3 tablespoons cider vinegar

3 tablespoons brown sugar

1 tablespoon fresh ginger, grated

Cheerful Chutney

Ginger has been proved to alleviate sinus and chest congestion, motion sickness, and nausea. This is a quick, easy chutney with an unusual flavor.

Preparation

Throw everything into a saucepan and boil until the berries pop and the texture is chutney-esque.

Serving Suggestion

Cook chutney together with your mother, your daughter, or another close female relative. Talk about when you were young. Try not to get on each other's nerves. Make memories. Then serve the chutney with the turkey and all the trimmings.

Buy yourself a gift.

Stressed Out

Stress is the disparity between the problem and a person's ability to cope with it. (What's stressful to you may not be to someone else. The difference between stress and stimulation is simply that you get to choose stimulation.) There are only two solutions for stress: either take away the cause (for example, get a different job), or help your mind survive (by using coping strategies such as meditation, deep breathing, or long weekends away—they're called vacations).

Look at what needs to change in your life. Explore ways you can simplify your routine, delegate tasks, and learn to say no to excessive demands. Eliminate recurring irritations whenever you can.

Stress is a problem when it produces symptoms in your behavior (such as sleep disturbances); your thought processes (negative, irrational thinking); your emotions (irritation), or your health (aches, pains, constant headaches). If you won't listen to your body, it will get your attention somehow.

Meditation is essential—but if the traditional, lotus-position kind doesn't appeal to you, try learning a new physical skill like dancing. Experiment until you find something totally absorbing. Losing

Maybe there's a reason your deadlines are always last-minute nightmares—stress can be as addictive as alcohol or nicotine: the adrenaline rush, the excitement, the sensation of being on a high.

yourself in the movement, the joy of surrendering your body to the rhythm, the mindlessness of "flow"—these are all pure meditation.

The easiest way to meditate is to go for a walk. Concentrate on your footsteps as you walk, or on the scenery, and let everything else go. Or, if you can't go outside, close your eyes and visualize the most soothing scene you can imagine. If you're thinking of a beach, listen to the waves crash, watch the palm trees sway. Really be there for five minutes, and take these little vacations whenever you need to.

Belly breathing is the easiest way to breathe for relaxation. Don't hold your tummy in, let it go in and out. Just take deep breaths, don't worry about doing it properly—you're stressed enough already!

People with strong relationships to others and social support get less stressed. If you're exercising, seeing friends, sleeping and eating properly, and you know that the stressful time won't last forever, you can cope with stress for a few months. The following strategies can help.

Congratulate yourself for finishing one job before you start the next. Try to achieve a balance between work and play during the week, so there's not so much pressure to cram all your living into the weekend.

You need balance, daily. If your job doesn't show concrete results, try to do something each day that gives instant gratification.

Establish transition routines to ease you into, or out of work. Be conscious of shifting gears. Take a nap, enjoy your garden. Get a massage, a back rub, or a hug. Go into a flower shop or a church for a few minutes. Try to shrug off all your cares for a little while each day so you remember what life should be like.

The healthier you are, the better you are able to cope with stress.

Over time, stress can drain the body of vitamins and minerals—

Prepare for stressful periods as much as you can in advance by being organized: have spares of things you'd be lost without, allow lots of time, eliminate clutter, learn yoga, have a stock of healthy meals in the freezer.

listen

magnesium and potassium in particular. Figs, pumpkin seeds, and seafood replace magnesium. Prunes, avocados, raisins, and bananas replace potassium.

One of the symptoms of stress is gastrointestinal problems. Digestion shuts down under stress, it's the flight-or-fight response. Refined, processed foods with preservatives, colorings, and additives place stress on your body because your liver has to work harder to detoxify them. The B vitamins (nuts, dark green leafy vegetables, wheat germ) and zinc (brown rice, bran, eggs, and oysters) have a calming effect on the digestion system.

If you're stressed, it's easy to eat too much too quickly. Be sure you're eating because you're hungry, not because you're upset.

Try This First

If you feel completely overwhelmed, the first thing you need to do is get control over your emotions. Then seek realistic ways to reduce the pressure. Get an extension on a deadline, get help, or get whatever it is you need to feel that you've done everything you could possibly do.

Identify what kind of pressure you're up against—it's the vague, nameless terror that's frightening. Is it a deadline? Is it worries about money? Write down exactly what's bothering you. When examined carefully, it might turn out that your stress is self-inflicted.

119

Thought to Chew on in the Kitchen

Is my job, or whatever is causing me anguish, worth the high blood pressure and heart attacks that stress leads to?

Stressless Lemon Cheesecake

When you are stressed, comfort foods from childhood with soothing textures like pudding help. Sweet things release mood-boosting endorphins to the brain. And when you're stressed, you don't need the hassle of juicing lemons and grating rind.

Maybe you can't take a real vacation, but you could take a vacation from something. Look at your life and see what you can cut out for six months. Then subtract something else at the end of the six months.

Ingredients

Cooking spray

⅓ cup crushed breakfast cereal,
  or plain, crumbly cookies like
  shortbread or graham crackers
  that have been crushed to
  make crumbs

2 eggs

15 ounces nonfat ricotta cheese

6 fluid ounces frozen lemonade
  concentrate, thawed (Store it in
  the refrigerator, not the freezer
  when you get it home from the
  supermarket. It must be cold
  when you use it, not room
  temperature.)

½ cup sugar

⅓ cup all-purpose flour

Preparation

Preheat oven to 350° F. Grease a 9-inch pie plate well with nonfat cooking spray.

Pour in the cereal or cracker crumbs to coat the pie plate. Tip out the excess.

In a large bowl, beat the eggs well with a fork, add the lemonade, sugar, and cheese and sift the flour on top. Mix well.

Pour this filling into the prepared pan. Bake 50 to 55 minutes, until the center is set and not wobbly.

Be patient! This cheesecake must be refrigerated for 2 or 3 hours before you eat it.

Serving Suggestion

A sliver of this cheesecake is a light snack with a creamy consistency that's comforting. Take with a cup of tea and think positive, calming thoughts while you eat. But also consider alternate ways to feel better, like getting a massage.

slow

Hurry Curry

Shrimp has about twice as much cholesterol as meat, but far less fat—and the fat it does have is mostly unsaturated. Shrimp also has a lot of good-for-bad-moods Omega-3 fatty acids.

This is a no-worry curry.

Preparation

Heat the oil in a large saucepan or Dutch oven and simmer the onion and curry powder until the onion is tender but not brown. Add the clam juice, salt, water, and rice, and bring the mixture to a low simmer. Cover and let cook for about 15 minutes or until the rice is done.

Add the sour cream and shrimp, and heat until everything is hot, but don't boil.

Serving Suggestion

If you're up for it, you could serve with all those little bits and pieces that traditionally come with curry—chopped peanuts, green onions, and so on. Otherwise, just serve with bottled mango chutney.

Ingredients

I teaspoon curry powder (or more, depending on how hot you want the dish to be)

½ cup chopped onion

I tablespoon canola oil

I 8-fluid ounce bottle of clam juice plus a half cup water

½ teaspoon salt

I cup raw long-grain rice

I cup sour cream

I cup pink, de-veined shrimp

down

The most stressful jobs have responsibility, but no authority.

> "I like work; it fascinates me. I can sit and look at it for hours."
>
> —Jerome K. Jerome

Fed Up with My Job

Don't waste your life doing anything less than what you love. You'll know it's what you are meant to do when you lose track of time doing it, when you feel connected to something larger than yourself.

If you are trying to find work that is completely in tune with who you are, and those "make a list of what you'd do if money was no object" exercises haven't worked, try this. As you move through your days, ask yourself at frequent intervals: What do I like about what I'm doing now? What do I hate? What activities do I always have time for, no matter how busy I am? What am I doing when I lose track of time?

Then think back to when you were first drawn to the kind of work you do now. When did you lose touch with that feeling?

Take time to explore these questions: Does my job bring out the best qualities in me? What percentage of my day is spent doing things I like? How do I feel at the end of the day? What have I accomplished that I can unashamedly boast about?

Or ask your true, good friends: How would you describe my type of energy? What sort of work do you think I should be doing? And recall how you were teased as a child—the accusations that made you

Know what success is—that is, what success means to you. What do you want out of life? But more important, how will you know when you get it?

performance

123

feel embarrassed. For example, you may have been chided for being "too sensitive." As an adult, your ideal career might be one where your sensitivity is an asset.

Why not take an evening-school course in anything even remotely interesting. It could become your next career.

You must dare to be who you genuinely *are* so you do the work that you were born to do. However long it takes to discover it—and it can take years—is time well spent.

And you will have discovered yourself in the process.

Try This First

If you hate your job, you have only three options: changing your attitude toward it, changing what's making the job unpleasant, or changing the job itself. Your first step is to decide which option you are going to take.

Your boss is not your mom, your coworkers are not your best friends. Your job doesn't keep you warm at night, your family and friends do.

Am I aligned with my purpose in life?

Cubicle Cuisine Sandwiches

Eating the right food for lunch can improve your mental energy, concentration, and performance for the rest of the day. High-protein meals help promote faster thinking and increased attention to detail.

Foods high in vitamin B6 (avocado, eggs, fish, prunes, molasses, spinach, peanuts) help the brain function better. Foods rich in boron—legumes; non-citrus fruits, such as apples, grapes, and pears; and cruciferous vegetables, like cabbage and broccoli; help to maintain mental alertness.

On a day you need to be performing at your peak, go for high-protein meals for mental clarity. Try sandwiches of:

- Chicken on whole wheat bread with a salad
- Pesto with tomato and mozzarella
- Hummus, chicken, and lemon juice
- Cream cheese, bananas, and raisins
- Guacamole and cheddar cheese

No time to make sandwiches? If you have sweet potatoes or yams in the kitchen, you have a quick, healthy, portable snack to take to work.

Have you noticed how some people who are afraid of being respected for who they are hide themselves behind their work so they'll be respected for what they do?

rest

At lunch time, buy plain salad greens at a takeout salad bar, then in the office kitchen wash the sweet potato (you can eat the skin, but you don't have to), prick it a couple of times with a fork, and put it on a paper napkin in the microwave. Bake on *high* for about 5 to 8 minutes, depending on how big it is. You can tell when it's done because you'll feel it give when you squeeze it (with your hand in an oven mitt). Scoop out the bright orange inside of the tuber onto the salad to add flavor and vitamin A. Eat with low-fat dressing.

You can do the same thing with regular potatoes, too. Keep a jar of salsa at work to spoon over them.

Serving Suggestion

The best drink to have with lunch at work? Water. Drinking endless cups of coffee is not a good idea. Drink coffee as an occasional treat, when you really need it.

The things you don't like about your career are also the things you don't like about yourself.

Don't measure success by your paycheck.

Brown-Bag Banana Bread

The health benefits of bananas change as they ripen. Firm, bright yellow bananas are a starchy food that give a gentle, lasting energy rise. In riper bananas, the starch has turned to sugar, a quick energy source.

Use very ripe, brown-speckled bananas, they're the sweetest and they'll make the bread more tender.

Preparation

Preheat oven to 350° F.

Mash the bananas in a large bowl. Mix in the eggs, oil, sugar, and walnuts thoroughly.

Sift the flour and baking soda directly into the bowl on top of the previous ingredients.

Stir—but not too thoroughly. Your goal is to beat as little as possible and yet get all the flour mixed in.

Pour into a greased 8½ x 4¼ x 3-inch loaf pan and bake at 350° F for 50 to 60 minutes.

Ingredients

3 ripe bananas (to make about a cup)

2 eggs

½ cup canola oil

½ cup sugar

1 cup chopped walnuts

1¼ cups whole wheat or plain flour

1 teaspoon baking soda

Serving Suggestion

Banana bread is a very portable afternoon treat. Have a slice with an apple or an orange to keep up your energy all day.

Having a Fat Day

Everyone has fat days, even stick-thin supermodels. And it has nothing to do with how many actual pounds you weigh.

You can feel fat because of water retention. Or medications: antihistamines, antidepressants, anti-inflammatories, and birth-control pills can affect fluid levels. Hormones also can account for all sorts of changes, and not just during your period. If you're tense, the stress hormone cortisol can cause fluid retention. Even humidity in the air can make your tissues retain water. But don't take diuretics, and don't avoid drinking water. When you're dehydrated, you become tired, which makes you feel hungry, when what you really need is H_2O.

If you have a bad body image, you need to be especially kind to yourself. Every time you think your arms look flabby, apologize to yourself and notice what you were thinking or feeling just before you had the negative thought. Hating the way you look is never about the way you look.

If you feel fine when you get up in the morning, then, during the day, decide that your thighs are huge, realize that it's not your thighs

It may be a fat day, but you could make it a good something-else day. Wear the most wonderful shoes you own, the ones that make you strut and feel great whenever you look down.

that are the problem. Something else—a work problem, perhaps—just added ten pounds for your psyche to worry about.

When you find fault with your body, you are finding fault with that part of our culture which objectifies women's bodies and makes them a critical part of her identity.

If you are really overweight, you may have learned to make food a tranquilizer when you're emotionally starved. For distressed babies, the most powerful comforter is food, and we continue to turn to it all through our lives. Reaching for a muffin is like trying to go home to a secure, safe place. If food was always served to you with a teaspoon of guilt—"I made this just for you," "You see how skinny she is, you'd think I never fed her," and vague references to starving hordes in India, Asia, or Europe, you may have developed negative emotions about food.

If you learn to tune in to your body's needs and only eat when you are really hungry, you won't need "willpower" to lose weight. When you are aware of your body and listen to what it's telling you, you will eat healthy food in moderation. If you're not tuned in, perhaps it's because you've battled your body image for so long that you are ignoring your actual body.

Exercise is a great way of making friends with it again. Working up a sweat by exercising helps minimize water retention. Don't focus on how many calories you're burning, think about what your body is doing and feeling. Remember when riding a bike was pure fun? When jumping rope with your girlfriends was play, not punishment for eating too much? That's the attitude toward exercise you want to regain. Exercise is a great time-out. It reduces the day's anxieties and burns off stress. Find a sport you want to excel at and keep yourself motivated by tracking your progress in a diary. Put on your favorite dance music

fine

The question is not whether you should exercise, but when and what kind.

129

and let yourself go. Walk the dog, jog with a friend, use your local park. Reward yourself whenever you reach a fitness goal.

Working out causes you to feel so much better afterwards. When you raise your heart rate, your brain increases production of feel-good endorphins. Only attempt to change your body shape for the right reasons: to get fit, to feel vital and alive, and to regain a sense of well-being.

Try This First

Have an emergency outfit to climb into on fat mornings—something very forgiving in the stomach region and flattering around your good points, with dark colors below the waist, and a bright color near your face.

Make your mantra for fat days: "It's a physical impossibility to put on ten pounds overnight." The formula doesn't change. If you take in more calories than you burn off, you'll gain weight.

Thought to Chew on in the Kitchen

Is my preoccupation with my body a way of hiding from other things that are making me miserable? If your life feels out of control, you might have decided that extra weight is the problem, rather than face up to the real difficulties.

Skinny Banana Cream Sorbet

Swim! Being submerged in water evens out the water pressure in your body.

Bananas contain a lot of potassium, which helps combat water retention and also helps control blood pressure and hypertension. They also help boost your serotonin and norepinephrine levels which naturally quells depression.

When bananas start to go brown, put them in the refrigerator—where they'll definitely go brown, but not rotten, and they'll still be good for lots of things, like banana bread or energy shakes. Or put them in the freezer tonight, so that tomorrow you'll only be a few minutes away from this sorbet.

Peel and cut two ripe bananas into chunks, place the pieces on a flat plastic lid or metal tray and put in the freezer, uncovered, until they're frozen hard like ice cubes.

Put the banana chunks in the blender with four generous tablespoons of fat-free vanilla yogurt. If the fruit just bounces around—and you'll be glad, now, if you have a powerful blender—add 2 tablespoons of orange juice or skim milk to help things along.

You might have to stop and redistribute the ingredients a bit, but this yummy, icy purée is definitely worth the few minutes it takes to blend, and this is a much easier method of making sorbet than fooling with an ice cream-making machine.

Taste and texture are best when semisoft, so serve immediately. This amount serves two people or one very hungry person.

You can also make this with any canned fruit. Keep a supply in the freezer to try. Fruit in heavy syrup is best—but don't freeze fruit in glass jars, they'll break! Transfer it to plastic containers first. Berries work, too. Separate and distribute over a flat surface like a cookie sheet and freeze uncovered.

Use about 1½ cups of fruit per person, with four large tablespoons of vanilla yogurt, plus two tablespoons of milk or juice, and blend.

Serving Suggestion

This sorbet makes a satisfying snack all by itself. It's mainly good-for-you, low-calorie, pure fruit.

On a fat day, you don't want to eat manufactured foods labeled "diet"—especially yogurt. They often contain ingredients designed to swell in the stomach to make you feel full. The sweeteners sorbitol and fructose also can cause bloating problems for some people.

Stand up straight and hold yourself with pride for a flatter stomach.

be kind

flattering

Ad Hoc Mock Guac

There's about 30 grams of fat in one avocado! If you're watching your weight, try this guacamole using asparagus, which contains no cholesterol and no fat.

Preparation

Drain the liquid from the can of asparagus. Rinse to wash off excess salt.

Put the asparagus, onion, cilantro, lime juice, and salt in the blender and purée. Pour into a bowl and fold in the sour cream and tomato.

Serving Suggestion

Just like regular guacamole, this tastes good on pita bread or crackers.

To avoid bloating, don't eat when you're upset or stressed. Avoid gas-inducing beans, and most prepared and packaged foods—they contain too much salt. Stay away from soda, especially with meals. Reduce caffeine and alcohol.

Ingredients

1 14-ounce can of asparagus cuts

⅓ cup chopped onion

2 tablespoons cilantro (coriander), no need to chop, just strip the leaves from the stems

1 tablespoon fresh lime juice

½ teaspoon salt

1 chopped fresh tomato, or 1 cup of chopped tomatoes

2 tablespoons fat-free sour cream

Can't Sleep

A satisfying night's sleep is one of life's great pleasures.

Severe sleep deprivation has the same symptoms as depression. When you're sleep-deprived, your good mood is the first thing to go—along with creativity, energy, memory, concentration, and coordination. Your stress hormone levels go up, and you lose sleep's power of fighting off sickness. Most of the body's growth and healing happens while you sleep—it may be the best thing we can do for ourselves.

Missing just a few hours of sleep on a regular basis accelerates aging by interfering with hormone production. Lack of sleep may actually lead to obesity—sleep deprivation can cause blood sugar levels to remain high after a meal, so your metabolism slows down.

You could probably improve the quality of your life by sleeping more. If you fall asleep immediately every night, that's a sign you're sleep-deprived. You may have been sleep-deprived for years. It takes about four weeks to reset your internal clock.

You know not to drink coffee or alcohol late in the evening, to try to get up at the same time every day, and to keep your bedroom cool, dark, and quiet. But have you considered you might possibly have a

A little night music: Bach's "Goldberg Variations" was commissioned to help an insomniac get to sleep.

sleep disorder, a lumpy mattress, or too much light entering your bedroom? Also, hormones—low progesterone—may keep women awake.

Studies show that light exercise in the early evening, combined with being exposed to bright light as soon as you wake up, provide all sorts of good effects on sleep patterns. But it's not the exercise, as such. It's the rise in body temperature, and then the cooling off which causes drowsiness. You could mimic the effect by taking a hot bath about two to three hours before bed.

Try a sleep ritual every night: lulling music, a warm bath, a soothing drink.

But what if you're doing everything right, yet still wake up with your mind racing over some gnawing problem at 4 A.M.? For most healthy people, difficulty falling asleep is usually due to stress. Your worried thoughts keep you awake. Throw them out! Before you go to bed, write down the problem, leave it on a table downstairs, and tell yourself you'll deal with it tomorrow. Wash the day's tensions off in the shower. Imagine picking up each little thought by the tail, as if it were an annoying little mouse, and flinging it far, far away. Find your own method. Just visualize it very clearly—and when your mind turns yet again to the fray, do it again, over and over, until you fall asleep.

Dreaming seems to be a way of digesting the day's experiences and consolidating memories. Do dreams mean anything? Maybe. Some dreams have obvious "meanings." (Dreaming of being naked is about revealing something and feeling vulnerable about it; flying is about getting away from the mundane details of existence.) Other dreams are more difficult to interpret.

Write down all you can remember about a dream as soon as you wake up, and try to focus on what role you played in the dream and your feelings about what happened. Emotions in dreams are honest

Sleep comes in waves every sixty to ninety minutes. If you are reading in bed and your eyes start to feel heavy, that's a wave. Don't try to finish the chapter, catch the wave.

reactions to events that are happening in your life. Don't worry too much about the individuals you dreamed about, look for a theme.

Rather than attempting to dredge up the "story" of the dream. For example, "I was in a big house"—ask yourself how you felt in the house. Scared? Lonely? Then explore what these feelings remind you of in your life when you're awake. And try describing what the elements of the dream mean to you. For example, if you dreamed of a swimming pool, think about what pools represent to you—fear, fun, a place where you would feel vulnerable, something to be kept clean? Ask yourself, why am I having this dream now?

Recurring dreams usually indicate an area that needs to be resolved. Being chased could symbolize fearing your own anger. Dreams can be shortcuts to your true feelings.

As you drift off to sleep, think about how you want the dream to end.

Try This First

Put on some socks. It is impossible to get to sleep with cold feet! Warming your feet makes the blood vessels dilate—the same thing melatonin does.

Are you relaxed? Tense up all your muscles, hold, then let it all go. Start with your feet, relax them, let them go limp. Then work your way up your body. Allow fingers, shoulders and jaw to relax.

Good-Night-Soon Snacks

Is there really a sleep/food connection? Yes! If you take foods which contain tryptophan (like milk and turkey) along with complex carbohydrates (like cereal, crackers, or bread), the sleep-inducing amino acid goes to the brain. The ideal time for a snack? Half an hour before bed.

Low levels of the B vitamins have been directly linked to sleepless nights. Insomnia depletes magnesium from the body, and low magnesium is linked with a lessened ability to deal with stress. Trace minerals like magnesium, zinc, iron, niacin, and copper, along with calcium, promote sleep. Too much aluminum can interrupt sleep. Make sure the antacid you take doesn't contain it. MSG, in meat tenderizers and Chinese food, can keep you awake, too.

But it's not so much what you eat at night but how much. After a big meal, the blood flow to the brain decreases and goes instead to your stomach to aid digestion. That's what makes you sleepy. To sleep well, eat dinner three or four hours before bedtime and avoid late night meals that are greasy, spicy, heavy, or high in protein.

Thought to Chew on in the Kitchen

Try to program your unconscious to work on problems while you're asleep. The idea is to fall asleep asking for the answer to something that's bothering you. Keep a pen and paper next to you on the nightstand, and write down whatever comes to mind first thing in the morning.

Or fall asleep focusing on someone who makes you feel good. Researchers have found it will put you in a good mood when you awake.

If you wake up unexpectedly in the middle of the night, don't check the clock. Quickly tell yourself to go back to sleep before you become too wide awake.

peace

- Combine a container of commercially made fat-free vanilla pudding with a cup of skim milk in the blender for a tasty bedtime drink.
- Or process a cup of skim milk with a banana in the blender. Sweeten if desired.
- Eat a few almonds—they contain tryptophan.
- Some people take a spoonful of ice cream every night before bed.
- Try herbal teas like chamomile or valerian.
- A little cereal with milk.
- Cheese or fruit and crackers.
- A low-fat oatmeal-raisin cookie.

Some people can bore themselves to sleep. Try doing something that is more of an effort than a pleasure for your brain: counting backward from one hundred, doing an acrostic crossword puzzle, watching a dull TV program.

Sweet Dream Pumpkin Cream Smoothie

Preparation

Whip up all the ingredients together in a blender.

Serving Suggestion

Take your before-bed snack after a warm bath, wrapped in a terry cloth robe that has been warmed in the dryer on the fluff cycle with a lavender-scented sachet. As you eat, envisage setting aside the worries of the day until tomorrow.

Ingredients

2 cups fat-free vanilla yogurt

¾ cup canned pumpkin (not pumpkin pie mix)

¾ cup skim milk

½ teaspoon each cinnamon, ginger, cloves, and nutmeg, or 2 teaspoons pumpkin pie spice

sleep

Too Busy to Enjoy Life

Feeling overwhelmed by your commitments signals a need to clarify your priorities. When the bulk of your time is spent doing things that reflect what you really believe in, you'll feel in control of your life and more satisfied with it.

Ask yourself: What is the right balance for me between work, rest, and play these days? Draw a pie chart of your time. The activities that bring you joy and fulfillment are the ones that really matter and these should occupy the most space on the chart.

Housework only deserves a small proportion of your time. For example, schedule all your chores and cleaning for Saturday. If something doesn't get done, tough. The rest of the week is yours to enjoy. Keep Sundays sacred: Decide to use the day to completely relax before the next week's madness starts.

Learn to delegate at work and at home. Hire a housekeeper when you're in a time crunch. See what errands you can take care of online—banking, grocery shopping, gift buying, travel planning, and bill paying are possibilities.

Do whatever you're doing with awareness. Focus on what you're doing right now this minute. Block out any thoughts of what you should do next or whether you did the last thing well enough. It's incredibly relaxing.

If you dismiss the idea of getting organized, perhaps there are other reasons behind your time-management failures. The frantically busy person often is running away from her demons.

Being busy can be a way of feeling worthwhile and needed. Arriving late is an old and common way to get attention. Making someone wait for something can be a way of controlling him. If you make sure your boss knows you feel overworked, you won't be given the extra pressure of more work. If you're "too busy" to make that call asking for something, you probably fear rejection.

Or maybe you secretly believe that if everything is organized and things are going smoothly, fate will intervene and something bad will happen. By being constantly busy, you can avoid getting close to someone. Leaving things until the last minute builds up high-adrenaline anxiety levels that can be stimulating and addictive. Defying the calendar or testing a deadline or losing your to-do lists can be an I'll-show-you gesture toward authority.

Do you recognize yourself yet?

When you know the real reasons your life is hectic, you'll know what to do about it.

Try This First

Everything that you are worried about is inside your head. You need to get it out of your head and onto paper so you can study the problem objectively and free your mind to decide what has to be done next. Make lists: Things I want to do. Things I need to do. People I should be connecting with.

Then break up the big things into manageable little chunks, and decide when to do them. Everything will feel less overwhelming when you've written it out.

power

Put your time where your heart is. Have no more than three major commitments in your life. They might be, for example, your family, your job, keeping fit.

141

Thought to Chew on in the Kitchen

What really counts in my life? Is there a way I can make that my first priority, every day?

PDQ Couscous

You're busy, but don't be tempted to skip meals—you need fuel for energy—or to grab a candy bar and coffee. Eat only when you're hungry, and go for complex carbohydrates low in fat, plus a little protein. Breakfast cereal with skim milk tastes good any time of day.

Couscous can't be beat for speed when you're coming to a boil but dinner isn't. It's a form of pasta made from semolina flour that will soften even if the liquid you soak it in is at room temperature. Get the whole wheat variety if you can find it. Use plain water or orange juice if you don't have chicken broth on hand.

Preparation

Pour the chicken broth into a saucepan. Cover and bring the liquid to a boil while you wrestle the frozen vegetables out of the ice in the freezer. Add to the boiling broth and simmer until they're heated through.

Pour in the couscous and stir. Keep the heat on until the liquid resumes boiling. Cover the saucepan and turn off the heat. Let it sit

Schedule pleasure. When something specific, like a half an hour at the library, is built into your schedule, you won't stress so much about the dirty kitchen floor.

142

day

Ingredients

¾ cup chicken broth

½ cup frozen mixed vegetables

½ cup couscous

optional: 1 or 2 tablespoons
  raisins or coarsely chopped
  dried apricots

for 5 minutes. If you have just a little more time, add some raisins or dried apricots to the broth as you heat it.

Serves one.

To serve more people: 1 cup of dry couscous with 1½ cups liquid will make 3¾ cups of grain and serve three to four people.

Serving Suggestion

Couscous with vegetables plus an energy shake will give you the fuel to do whatever it is you have to do.

Notice how your food smells, its texture and flavor. Taste the colors. Eat slowly, appreciating the nourishment you are getting. Make sure you chew each mouthful properly. Bring to meals a consciousness and appreciation for the food on your plate.

When you're finished, signal to yourself that the meal is over by brushing your teeth or drinking tea, rather than continuing to nibble mindlessly through the day.

*The only power you have is
to make the most of
every single day.*

*Don't move so quickly that
you miss your own life.*

143

Quick Bean Burrito Wraps for Two

Preparation

Each tortilla gets half the beans, cheese, onion, and cilantro arranged on top of it. Then fold the four sides of the tortilla into the center, overlapping them. Wrap each burrito in a slightly dampened paper towel.

Place seam side down on a microwave-safe plate. Microwave on *high* for about 4 minutes, serve with the salsa and sour cream.

Serving Suggestion

A burrito plus gazpacho to drink makes a satisfying meal. Try not to have any distractions from your food. If you really can't get out of the office, try facing in a different direction while you eat, or at least covering up your work.

Before you start eating, take a few long, deliberate breaths. Don't gobble your food, no matter how busy you are. Eat mindfully. Food isn't—or shouldn't be—just functional fuel. It's our connection to life.

Ingredients

2 low-fat whole-wheat or regular 10-inch flour tortillas

2 tablespoons black beans or pinto beans from a can

¼ cup shredded Monterey Jack or cheddar cheese

1 sliced green onion

4 tablespoons cilantro (also known as coriander or Chinese parsley), chopped

2 tablespoon store-bought chunky-style salsa

2 tablespoons fat-free sour cream

Other Easy, Healthy Meals

- Wash a baked potato. Pierce it a couple of times with a fork, put it on a paper towel in the microwave and zap for about 8 minutes—you'll know it's done when you squeeze it with an oven mitt on your hand and feel it give. Make a deep X on one side with a knife, open up the potato and fill with plain fat-free yogurt and chives.

- Toasted pita bread topped with tomato or spaghetti sauce, low-fat mozzarella cheese, and fresh chopped peppers makes a mini pizza.

- Canned tuna or salmon mixed with low-fat mayonnaise or low-fat sour cream and chopped sweet pickles or capers on crisp bread.

- Try other canned seafood: toss crab into a salad or serve over pasta or in omelettes. Sardines packed in water make a good sandwich with tomato ketchup.

- Look in the deli for precooked meats, cheeses, and roasted vegetables that can be combined with cooked pasta or become part of an antipasto platter.

Serving Suggestion

You need plenty of liquids so you don't get tired. Instead of coffee, eat an orange with your quick meal. It's 87 percent water. Or a grapefruit—that's about 8 ounces of water. When you eat fruit instead of a commercial fruit drink, you get the added benefit of real vitamins and minerals.

Don't eat on the run, in front of the television, or at your desk! It's bad for the digestion and for your soul. Set a timer and make yourself take at least half an hour for lunch.

Drowning in Clutter

Having an overabundance of *stuff* can be stressful—acquiring and caring for possessions can waste a lot of time, obstruct your thinking, and obscure the true values of life.

But, before you start cleaning out your closets, you need to get yourself into the right frame of mind. You need to acknowledge the abundance you have. You need to acknowledge that you have changed over the years and that you no longer need things that were once essential. When you give up something at age forty, you aren't taking it away from your twenty-one-year-old self who needed it way back when. You also need to realize that when you get rid of something, you are opening the way for new and better things.

Now you are ready to clear the clutter and cleanse your soul.

The temptation, when clearing clutter, is simply to find new places to put things. But moving stuff from closet to closet is not the solution. You need to toss, donate, or recycle.

When you long for a specific item you don't have, visualize buying it and loving it—but then also visualize yourself getting tired of it and throwing it away. You may find you don't need to buy it.

Clarify your personal goals. Then, when it's time to make decisions about different objects, you can aim to clear a path toward that goal by getting rid of the things that don't contribute to it.

essentials

Ask these questions of each item:

• What does this help me accomplish?

• How easy would it be to replace this?

• Can it be replaced for under $10?

• Could someone else use and enjoy this?

• If I'm keeping something in case I want to use it in a few years time, will this be what I want? If you ever take up rowing again, won't you want a newer boat, better oars?

Interview each object. Ask it what it's doing in your space and where it belongs.

Save only the best of your collections. Take a photo of an item and save that instead. Have those baby shoes bronzed for bookends. Frame the scarf you love but never wear.

Keep only the clothes that make you feel wonderful. The ordinary clothes stay ordinary, but the outstanding stay outstanding. If you get rid of the nonessentials, then the essentials will have a chance to shine.

When you're done, you will have cleared your life and your mind.

A continual need to acquire objects often masks a need to fill an emotional void. But emotional voids don't get filled this way.

Why do I need to acquire so many material possessions? What void am I trying to fill? If I absolutely cannot do away with attachments, why not attach myself to the good things in life—love, laughter, memories?

Clean-Out-the-Cans Bean Salad

Clean out your kitchen cupboard by making a multi-bean salad that uses up all those cans! Beans have plenty of folate, which helps fight the effects of stress.

Don't eat beans much because you can't be bothered finding out what to do with each kind? Don't worry—you don't have to know which is which to get the nutritional benefits! Just throw a selection of different cans in your supermarket cart and make a salad.

If you are not enjoying life with the possessions you have now, having more won't help.

out

Ingredients

- 1 7-ounce can of whole kernel corn

- 2 10-ounce cans of any of these bean varieties: black, red, lima, white kidney, or chickpeas

- 1 red bell pepper

- 1 9-ounce package frozen cut green beans

- 1 tablespoon chopped fresh cilantro

- 1 16-ounce jar of sweet mixed pickles (You're only going to use the liquid for this recipe. Refrigerate the pickles, later you can chop them up for Sea Change Tuna Salad. Simplifying life isn't necessarily a simple process.)

Preparation

Get out the can opener and get to work.

Chop up the bell pepper.

Heat the green beans in the microwave, on high, for about 4 to 5 minutes.

Combine everything in a large salad bowl.

Marinate the whole lot in the liquid from the jar of sweet mixed pickles.

Serving Suggestion

Take a break from tidying up and have the bean salad with some bread. Beans plus whole wheat bread make a complete protein.

And while you're in the kitchen, empty the cupboards of empty calories—soda, sweets, oils, and fats. You deserve better than junk food.

A mess is a tangle of postponed decisions.

Use-Up-the-Bread Pudding

When you read the words "unbleached" and "enriched" on the bag, white bread often seems to be as nutritious as brown, but in fact, the healthiest bread to buy will have "whole wheat" listed as the first ingredient in the nutrition facts box.

Eggs are a great source of iron, protein, and vitamins A and E. Just don't eat more than four yolks a week.

Stale or dry bread is best since much of the moisture has evaporated, so bread can soak up flavored cream. Any bread will do, you can store leftovers in the freezer until you have enough for a pudding. Whole wheat is best for nutrition, but brioche and challah taste awfully good.

Eliminate what you're not and what's left will be you.

Preparation

Spray a 7-inch soufflé dish or casserole with nonstick spray.

Tear up the bread into small chunks, and put into the dish. Sprinkle the golden raisins throughout the chunks of bread.

In a separate bowl, beat the eggs, then add the milk, syrup, sugar, cinnamon, and nutmeg. Mix well. Pour over the bread and golden

organize

raisins. Press down. Let stand for at least half an hour. The longer it stands, the more soufflé-like the pudding becomes. Soak very hard bread until it's completely soft. (It can stay overnight in the refrigerator.)

Bake in a preheated 350° F oven for 35 to 40 minutes, or until set. If the first spoonful reveals a runny, liquid interior, put the pudding back in the oven for a few minutes longer.

Bread pudding is good eaten hot or cold.

Serving Suggestion

When you clean out your refrigerator, make a salad to use up the vegetables, then have bread pudding as a substantial, comforting dessert, served with low-fat vanilla yogurt if you like.

Next time, store fruit and vegetables in clear plastic containers at eye level instead of in the crisper where you'll forget about them. Put leftovers in the freezer immediately after dinner, so you aren't tempted to keep snacking all evening. Store chocolate there, too.

Throw out the ancient baking soda and baking powder—they won't work as well as fresh. Those decades-old dried herbs and spices can all get tossed, too—they lose their punch after a few months.

Ingredients

6 to 7 slices of bread, or enough odds and ends of bread to almost fill an 7-inch round soufflé dish

1 cup golden raisins

2 eggs

1½ cups skim milk (For a richer taste, you can use evaporated skim milk, or combine it with skim milk in any proportion, as long as there's a total of 1½ cups.)

⅓ cup maple syrup or molasses

¼ cup sugar

¼ teaspoon cinnamon

¼ teaspoon nutmeg

> "What, after all, is a halo? Only one more thing to keep clean."
>
> —Christopher Fry

Wanting Everything to Be Perfect

A person driven by the desire to do well and stressed from the fear of failure is carrying a heavy load—not to mention wasting time on things that don't matter.

What do you gain by being a perfectionist? Perhaps it's a way of feeling good about yourself, or a way to distance yourself from others.

And, if your parents were never satisfied with what you achieved, you probably grew up being dissatisfied with yourself. Now you're an adult, other people are too caught up in their own problems to notice your mistakes. Today, you are the only dissatisfied person.

Perfection is an illusion. You can decide only what is perfect by comparing it to something else and keeping score. But life is constantly changing. Become comfortable with instability and you set yourself free from perfectionism.

Realize that something imperfect can be more meaningful than something perfect. Potato-print wrapping paper made by the kids is

Is this task really worth doing well? Give yourself permission to give, say, a gift certificate instead of searching for the right gift, to serve frozen meals, to skip the nonessentials.

appreciated by their grandparents much more than perfect, color-coordinated packages with camera-ready bows, and it's more fun for everyone. Beware of caring more for order than for people.

To heal yourself, create a coping dialogue, or mantra. For example: "Doing things right is not as important as doing the right things."

Take risks without worrying about the outcome. Mistakes are how we learn.

Make a mess. Get your fingers dirty. Separate eggs with your fingers. Mix meatloaf with your hands. Enjoy the disorder. Life is messy. Cooking—and passion—aren't neat.

Try This First

Giving up perfectionism requires a fundamental shift in your attitude toward yourself. You must let go of the idea that your worth is determined by your achievements and accomplishments.

Did you have a chaotic childhood? Consider that your obsession with perfection may be the way you're still striving to gain control of things and get order in your life.

Does what I'm doing really have
to be this complicated? How important will any of this be five years
from now?

Almost Perfect Almost Alfredo Pasta Sauce

Perfectionism can be stressful. For a calm, focused mind, eat complex carbohydrates such as whole grain bread and pasta dishes.

But, there's no need to make perfect pasta sauce from scratch! Let someone else chop the garlic.

In the onion-dip intensive 1950s, cookbooks were full of recipes using canned soups as sauces—nice try, but somehow they tasted of powdered garlic and MSG. This recipe uses a commercially made product, too, but one that's light, cheesy, and delicious.

The problem is not in having high standards or working hard, but in feeling driven, living a life that keeps you from being happy.

almost

Ingredients

½ pound dry pasta (broad pastas work best: fettuccine or noodles)

125 grams (4.4 ounces) light Boursin cheese (Choose whichever flavor you prefer—garlic and fine herbs works well.)

¼ cup evaporated skim milk

8 ounces low-fat cottage cheese

4 or 5 sprigs of parsley (You don't have to chop them, just strip the leaves off the stems.)

Preparation

Cook the pasta according to package directions.

While it's cooking, put the other ingredients in the blender and whirl them up—that's all there is to it! If you pour this sauce over the freshly cooked pasta, hot and steaming, you won't have to heat the sauce.

Serving Suggestion

Try some green tea with the pasta. It's the perfect drink for perfectionists: it has no calories and contains cancer-fighting antioxidants called polyphenols, potent free radical fighters.

Dolce Vita Desserts

Perfectionism is one of the strongest risk factors for developing an eating disorder. Because food is one of the few things you can control in life, you can turn it into a weapon. Perfectionists often believe they have to follow an eating plan exactly or not at all. Not true—small changes in your diet are better than no changes.

Don't let food control you. Eat sweets that are healthy, rather than trying to eliminate all sweets. And the perfect dessert doesn't have to take long to make.

OK, lemon curd and peanut butter have a lot of fat—but the rest of the suggestions here are very healthy, and all are triumphs of awesome simplicity.

- Spoon a dollop of chunky apple sauce over low-fat ice cream.
- Mix a half cup of plain, canned pumpkin with a cup of low-fat vanilla yogurt, add a dash of cinnamon and nutmeg.
- Take a cup of plain cottage cheese, fold in a half cup of lemon curd, and scatter some blueberries on top. (You'll find lemon curd near the jams in the supermarket. If you like lemon chiffon pies you'll like this—it's the lemon custard part in a jar.)

Concentrate on the task, not on the outcome.

- Shake some instant coffee granules over low-fat coffee ice cream.

- Stir one tablespoon of chunky peanut butter into a container of prepared, fat-free chocolate pudding (usually near milk in the supermarket) and warm gently in a saucepan (don't boil). Pour over low-fat vanilla ice cream and sliced bananas.

- Sprinkle thick slices of pineapple with brown sugar. Broil in the toaster oven for three minutes until the sugar caramelizes.

- Fast fruit fondue: Cut up fresh fruit for dunking in fat-free chocolate syrup.

- Mix two cups of low-fat sour cream with a cup of cherry jam and two tablespoons of cherry brandy. Freeze for 30 minutes only—you want it icy but not frozen solid.

- If you keep a few different types of dried fruits soaking in the refrigerator they'll keep for at least a week or so, and make a good fast snack any time of the day. (Try with cereal for breakfast.) Get a bag of mixed fruits: apples, pears, apricots, and peaches. And don't avoid pitted prunes—they are one of the best antioxidants. Put the fruit in a ceramic or glass bowl (not aluminum) and cover with boiling water (toss in a tea bag, such as ginger or green tea for added flavor and nutrients). Once the bowl cools, store in the refrigerator to soak overnight. The next day, eat cold or warm in the microwave and serve with fat-free vanilla yogurt.

- Make baked apples—this is a good way of using fruit that turns out to be hard as a bullet, or unappetizingly mushy and soft when you get it home from the market. Choose a mild to slightly tart variety of apple: Cortland, Golden Delicious, Granny Smith, Newtown Pippin, Rome Beauty, Jonathan, or Greening. Wash the apples, then use a long, thin knife to cut out the core. The goal is to leave the apple intact except for a hole through the middle. If the apple does

passion

not stand up on its own, cut a thin slice off the bottom so it will. Place in a microwave-safe baking dish and stuff the center with a teaspoonful of brown sugar or maple syrup, plus a tablespoonful of raisins or chopped dried apricots and walnuts. Or, you could try apple butter, cranberry sauce, or chopped crystallized ginger—whatever's at hand.

A little liquid dribbled over the apples keeps them from drying out. Use two to three tablespoons to a half cup of any of the following: orange juice, apple juice, calvados, applejack, apple cider, rum, brandy cognac.

Microwave on *high* for 10 minutes or until the apples are soft—test by poking a fork into the side. Serve with low-fat yogurt.

Serving Suggestion

Channel your perfectionist tendencies into presenting the dessert beautifully—garnish with a perfect strawberry or arrange the components with Zen precision—to heighten the pleasure of the meal.

No, you're not perfect. Thank goodness! Better than that, you're unique.

Feeling Poor

Money *does* buy happiness. Being financially comfortable increases our choices and allows us freedom to work toward self-growth and creativity. But once the basics have been satisfied, it's our attitude to money that's more important than how much we have.

If you think you'd be content with just a little more, but keep measuring your worth by comparing what you have to what others have, you will never be content.

As Quentin Crisp advised, don't try to keep up with the Joneses. Drag them down to your level. It's cheaper.

There are two ways of being rich—to be very wealthy or to be content with what you have.

The biggest obstacle to a full life isn't lack of money, it's fear. It's not who you are that holds you back, but what you think you're not. Act like a poor person and that's what you are. There's no security in life, only opportunities.

If you don't like what is happening in your life—the effect—look at what you are doing—the cause. The only person standing

Am I making a distinction between inner and outer obstacles? Is it spiritual nourishment I need, or just an un-maxed-out credit card? What do I need to feel fully alive right now? How can I fill this void spiritually, intellectually, physically? If a problem can be solved with money, it's not a problem.

content

in your way to a better life is you. Ask yourself: "What am I doing to prevent my friends, the company I work for, my parents, my spouse, from giving me what I want?"

If you focus wholeheartedly and exclusively on something, you'll eventually attract it to you. The only difficulty is finding what it is you really want. The only success is being able to spend life growing, learning, and enjoying the process. Most people strive for comfort and luxury when all we really need to make us happy is something to be enthusiastic about.

Try This First

Life Appreciation 101: Live in the moment. Appreciate the mundane. All we have is this moment, right now.

Check out the first-class route whenever you can—you may decide not to take it, but why feel deprived by assuming you can't?

What does money represent to me? Power? A measure of my worth? A nuisance? Freedom? How you think about money—how you use it, spend it and save it—is a metaphor for how you feel about yourself.

Eggplant Caviar

Enjoying life means not wishing you had real caviar, but enjoying food.

As artist Paul Gauguin said, "No mean woman can cook well, for it calls for a light head, a generous spirit, and a large heart."

Eggplant is low in calories and sodium, high in fiber, and it may lower cholesterol. Garlic contains selenium, a natural immune system booster.

Quality of life doesn't depend on where you are living, but on who you are being.

Money can be taken from you at any time, but wealth is yours forever. Be greedy for all the good things in life: love, laughter, friendship.

enjoying

Ingredients

2 eggplants, about 2 pounds in all
(An eggplant should be heavy
for its size, feel like a rubber
ball, and have a round, not oval,
scar on the bottom.)

4 garlic cloves

1 teaspoon soy sauce

4 tablespoons best quality olive
oil

salt, pepper

¼ cup currants

¼ cup toasted pine nuts or walnut
pieces

Preparation

Prick the eggplants several times with a fork and place in the microwave. Cook on high for about 10 minutes until soft and collapsed, or bake them, cut in half, in a preheated oven, 350° F for 1 hour. (You can toast the pine nuts or walnuts on a flat cookie sheet at the same time, for better flavor, but it's not essential.)

When the eggplants are cool, squeeze gently over the sink to extract the excess liquid.

Scrape out the eggplant flesh into the blender. Add the garlic, oil, seasoning, and soy sauce and process.

This can be refrigerated overnight, but add the currants and nuts at the last moment.

Serving Suggestion

This spread is excellent on crisp dry toast or hot pita bread. Drink bubbly water with a wedge of lime—a cleaner, fresher taste than champagne. Living well means reveling in the sensual pleasure of eating foods that are good for you.

Use the good china every day—
why postpone the good
things in life?

162

Breakfast-Like-a-King French Toast

Helen Gurley Brown says that sex, sleep, and food are joys not enjoyed by rich people any more than by poor people, and she's right.

Anybody can have a more cheerful and energetic morning if they eat a low-fat, high carbohydrate breakfast. Many people don't eat breakfast—that's a big mistake. Going without food for 14 hours puts you at risk of gallstones. You also lower your problem-solving abilities when you have low blood-sugar levels—not a good way to start the day.

Preparation

Spray a large baking sheet with nonstick spray. Preheat the oven to 450° F.

In a blender, whirl the milk, bananas, flour, and cinnamon until smooth.

Pour into a shallow bowl.

Dip the bread into the mixture, turning to coat both sides. Allow to soak for a few minutes. Place on baking sheet.

Bake in 450°F oven for 6 minutes or until bread is lightly browned. Turn over and bake for 5 to 8 minutes more.

Ingredients

⅓ cup skim milk

1 mashed banana

4 teaspoons whole wheat flour

¼ teaspoon ground cinnamon

2 slices whole wheat bread

Serving Suggestion

Sprinkle with nutmeg or cinnamon sugar, or serve with real maple syrup. Drink decaf coffee, herb tea, or grapefruit juice.

Breakfast-Like-a-King Pancakes

Preparation

Combine flour, oats, cinnamon, baking powder, and salt in a large bowl. Mix in buttermilk, oil, and egg yolks.

In an unlined copper bowl, beat the egg whites until stiff. (See "Cooling-Off Cold Grapefruit Soufflé" for how to do this.)

Spray a nonstick frying pan with cooking spray. Heat the pan for about a minute. When it's hot, pour in one-quarter cup of batter. Cook about 90 seconds, until edges bubble, then flip with a spatula and cook the other side. The second side takes less time, only about 20 seconds.

Repeat until you've used up all the batter.

Serve with real maple syrup or fresh fruit.

Ingredients

1 cup all-purpose flour

½ cup quick-cooking rolled oats, not instant

½ teaspoon cinnamon

1 tablespoon baking powder

½ teaspoon salt

1½ cups buttermilk

2 tablespoons canola oil

2 large eggs, separated (eggs separate best when cold, whip best when room temperature)

wealth

spiritually

Blueberry Pancakes

Preparation

Mix the flours, baking powder, baking soda, and sugar in a large bowl.

Add the egg white and apple juice. Stir, then fold in the blueberries.

Spray a nonstick frying pan with cooking spray. Heat the pan for about a minute. When it's hot, pour in one-quarter cup of batter. Cook about 90 seconds, until edges bubble, then flip with a spatula and cook the other side. The second side takes less time, only about 20 seconds.

Repeat until you've used up all the batter.

Serve with real maple syrup or fresh fruit.

Serving Suggestion

The ideal breakfast is a little lean protein, such as yogurt, with the complex carbohydrates in the French toast or pancakes, for maximum alertness. Or have a cappuccino: skim milk has protein. If you spend a small fortune on take-out caffeine treats, buying a coffee maker could save you money.

Ingredients

¾ cup whole wheat pastry flour

½ cup all-purpose flour

2 teaspoons baking powder

¼ teaspoon baking soda

2 tablespoons sugar

1 egg white, beaten until frothy with a fork

¾ cup apple juice

1 cup fresh blueberries

work
out

Low Voltage Vitality

"Life begets life. Energy creates energy. It is by spending oneself that one becomes rich."

—Sarah Bernhardt

If your lack of energy is unremitting, you may have a medical problem—anemia, thyroid problems, or chronic fatigue syndrome. Go see your doctor.

Iron deficiency can make you exhausted for months. About 25 percent of the general public and up to 80 percent of exercising women are iron deficient. Anemia is the final stage. Have a blood test if you think your tiredness may be caused by lack of iron in your diet.

At least once a day, eat an iron-rich food such as fortified cereal, spinach, or red meat. Ideally, you should eat small amounts of lean meat and larger amounts of iron-rich grains. Increase your intake of fruits and vegetables—their vitamin C will help your body use the iron in plant foods. Make sure you're getting enough B vitamins, iron, and magnesium.

Energy ebbs and flows in daily, monthly, and seasonal waves. But the more your conscious goals are aligned with your innermost wants and desires, the greater energy you'll have. This is what spurs people to expend the superhuman effort needed to achieve extraordinary feats.

Don't underestimate what a renewable resource your energy is. After a tiring day, you may not be able to get yourself interested in cleaning out a closet, but if a friend came up with tickets to something you wanted to see, you'd have vitality to spare. Feelings are what give you energy.

Know the times of day you're most productive and least tense—plan your activities accordingly. Be aware of your body—sleep, amount of physical activity, diet, and health are all connected. A lethargic mood often can be traced back to one of these variables.

Exercise! The worse you feel before a workout, the better you will feel afterwards. It gives you so much—a release from stress, better sleep, a natural high from endorphins. It'll strengthen your bones, improve your skin, and burn calories overtime.

But the best benefit is the way it makes you feel good. Studies have shown that depressed people who do aerobics can improve their mood as much as people taking anti-depressant drugs.

At the very least, stretch every day to increase blood supply to your muscles.

Try This First

This is a tried and true series of energy boosters, but be sure to do each step (find alternatives if you have to).

1. Go to a bathroom and run cold water over your wrists. (Splash cold water on your face, too, if you can. Drinking something icy is also effective.)

2. Brush your hair, preferably with one of those scalp-massaging brushes with little rubber nodules on the end of each bristle.

3. Suck a peppermint, as much for the smell as the taste. Or, peel open an orange and sniff. Any citrus rind will give you a lift. Or splash on a revitalizing cologne—jasmine is a picker-upper.

4. Bend over and touch your toes, it revs up your circulation—or go for a walk around the block to get some sun and fresh air.

5. Look at something brightly colored to perk up your brain. A good excuse to buy flowers for your desk!

6. Breathe deeply.

Sit up straight. Your body has to work twice as hard when it's not aligned properly. Deep breathing delivers more oxygen to "the blood. Take fewer, deeper breaths.

Get energy by connecting with living things—get a dog or cat.

grow

Is this lack of energy physical or mental? If you've lost your energy suddenly, and if you feel tired all the time, see a doctor. If something you are worried about is sapping your vitality, you need to address the problem.

Energy in a Glass I

For a steady source of energy throughout the day, you need to keep blood sugar levels steady: eat small meals every two or three hours. And even low-level dehydration can deplete your energy, so keep drinking water throughout the day or drink a snack, like this smoothie.

One banana + one cup of low-fat or fat-free yogurt + half a cup orange juice + five or six strawberries = one great drink when whirled in the blender.

Serving Suggestion

Eat a food that has boron—such as an apple, or grapes—with the shake to help maintain mental alertness. Or, for a more substantial snack, try a smear of peanut butter on whole wheat bread. The combination of carbohydrates, protein, and some fat, is ideal because each is digested at a different rate.

Lack of sunlight may be sapping your energy. Get outside, especially in winter, even if it's overcast. Exposure to sunlight increases production of serotonin (a feel-good chemical) and norepinephrine, a hormone that increases alertness.

Energy in a Glass II

The fruit from a small papaya, a mango, or 2 peaches + 3 table-spoons fat-free sweetened condensed milk + the juice from half a lime + cold water = a great milk shake when whirled in the blender.

Serving Suggestion

For a quick spurt of energy, eat raisins or something sweet with the shake. For a steadier stream of energy, eat pasta or whole-meal cookies. But avoid large, high-fat meals. To digest the fat, your body diverts blood away from your brain and muscles—you'll feel sluggish.

Have a light snack, then spend your lunch hour at the gym.

Your body burns about 15 percent more calories if you exercise after a meal than if you work out before. But don't exercise right after a heavy, high-fat meal, or else your muscles will compete with your stomach for blood flow. Wait at least an hour.

Have you ever experienced the "helper's high" you get when you give of yourself? You don't need to volunteer at the local hospital—it works on a smaller scale, too. Try small doses, like helping a mother with a baby carriage up the escalator, or holding open doors.

identify

Too Many Bad Habits

To work with an athlete effectively, a good coach listens attentively—thereby knowing when to push and when to suggest an afternoon off. The coach tells the athlete what to do in a way she needs to hear it.

If you pay attention to yourself, you'll learn how to get out of your own way so you can work with your mind and body the way a coach would. When you are on your own side, you still have fears, but you've made friends with them.

When you can't make your body do what you want, your subconscious is initiating self-defeating behavior to keep you from achieving your conscious goals.

Identify the fear behind your self-sabotaging behavior so you can deal with it. For example, if you lost weight you might subconsciously fear having to cope with attention from men, and you're not sure how to handle that.

Do you procrastinate? You may be procrastinating as rebellion against daily activities that don't reflect the values you believe in.

If you are a workaholic, ask yourself what's threatening about being at home. Stress of the job might be a a distraction from a difficult relationship.

Ask yourself: Am I doing the things that are really, really important to me? Procrastination can be a way of trying to control situations.

If resentment, anger, or rebellion is preventing you from starting a task, tackle the causes of those feelings—separate the emotion from the task itself.

Or, perhaps you're addicted to being late. Pushing deadlines can provide an adrenaline rush—it's actually a type of gambling.

To get yourself to do a big, formidable task, make molehills out of mountains: Divide it into manageable bits and reward yourself after each—even if it's as simple as a single jelly bean after each phone call.

To get yourself to take up a good habit, first, vividly imagine the results. Then consciously commit to the change. Tell everyone what you're doing. The more you talk about it, the more obligated you'll be to do it.

Begin behaving like the person you want to be, even if it feels strange. Hook the new behavior onto something that's already a habit, if necessary. Notice the benefits of the change and use these positive feelings to motivate yourself further. Eventually, the change will feel natural. It takes three to six months for new behavior to stick. Be patient.

To get rid of a bad habit, try consciously performing the habit a few times as you tell yourself emphatically that you won't be doing it anymore.

And, make sure you're doing it for yourself, not just because you want to please someone else. You must be really ready to quit. Only try to change one bad habit at a time.

If you backslide, start over again. And again.

Try This First

Try giving up your bad habit for just two weeks. See if you can handle a temporary time out.

Bribe yourself as an incentive to get going on tasks you don't want to do.

start over

natural

Caffeine-Freak Trifle

If too much coffee is one of your bad habits, know that it's not something you must give up completely. Yes, more than 1,000 milligrams of coffee a day, or 8 cups, can produce symptoms of nervous irritability, headache, and heart rate problems. Plus, coffee is a diuretic, it takes water out of your body, which can make you tired. And coffee and tea contain tannins that reduce the effect of nutrients you need, like calcium and iron.

But it does have a few redeeming virtues.

Caffeine inhibits the nerve chemical adenosine that blocks energy-boosting brain chemicals. A cup of coffee or soda can ease headaches by constricting blood vessels. And the latest news about coffee is that it boosts cells in the hippocampus, stimulating new branches to develop. Also, several of its ingredients may help block some of the damage caused by free radicals, responsible for many of the signs of aging. There's some evidence it may decrease the risk of developing Parkinson's disease, give you a short-term energy boost, and elevate your mood.

This is something like the Italian dessert *Tiramisu*, without the delicious—but fattening—marscapone cheese.

Be self-centered enough to care about your body by giving it just enough best-quality food.

living things

Ingredients

1 8-ounce container of low-fat cottage cheese

1 8-ounce container of low-fat vanilla yogurt

3 tablespoons sugar

½ teaspoons vanilla

5 ounces fat-free pound cake

3 tablespoons very strong coffee

2 tablespoons sweet Marsala liqueur

1 ounce semi-sweet chocolate

powdered cocoa

Preparation

In a blender or food processor, combine the cottage cheese, yogurt, sugar, and vanilla.

Take 4 dishes. In each, place a slice of cake, pour over some of the coffee and liqueur, and top with cottage cheese mixture and some grated chocolate. Dust top with powdered cocoa.

Serving Suggestion

Treat yourself to trifle after a light meal of soup or salad. And when you're alone, take up one of the best bad habits: read while you eat. That way, you get to choose who'll keep you company, you don't have to make small talk, and there's no one to disapprove when you dribble stew down your T-shirt.

Or eat in front of TV. You can't be perfect all the time.

Super Supermarket Lamb Stew

This stew is easy to put together because you buy the vegetables already prepared. Does this mean they're not as good for you? Not necessarily. Sometimes, canned and frozen foods actually provide more nutrition than their fresh counterparts. When fruits and vegetables are frozen, nutrient loss is usually less than 20 percent, while fresh produce can lose up to 60 percent just in the time it takes to get to the store.

Get into the habit of fruit and vegetables from whatever sources are most readily available, rather than on relying on fast food.

Stews always taste better the next day, when the flavors have had a chance to mingle.

Start doing the thing you've been resisting first thing in the morning, or you'll ruin the whole day by dreading it.

Preparation

Cut the meat into one-inch square cubes. (At this size, they cook quicker and become more tender than the usual, larger, 2-inch squares most recipes call for.)

In a large casserole with a lid, or Dutch oven, sear the meat cubes in the oil until they're brown. Add all the other ingredients except the peas, cover, and simmer at the lowest possible heat for an hour.

Take out a piece of meat and taste it. If it is tender, add the peas and heat until they are done.

Serving Suggestion

Drink a glass of red wine with the stew, even if it means opening a new bottle just for yourself. Red wine is full of the antioxidant resveratrol—a limited amount can be part of a healthy diet.

Ingredients

1½ pounds lean stewing lamb (Don't buy meat whose only claim to fame is that it is government inspected. All meat should be. Find meat labeled USDA choice—or USDA prime if you can get it.)

¼ cup olive oil

1 10-ounce box of frozen pearl onions

1 1-pound bag of peeled baby carrots

1 11-ounce can low-fat tomato soup

1 11-ounce can low-fat chicken broth

1 cup raw long-grain rice

1 tablespoons Worcestershire sauce

½ teaspoon salt

1 8-ounce packet of frozen peas

important

Super Supermarket Fish Stew

Eating oily fish regularly is one of the best ways to eat for health—a wide range of health benefits have been linked to the Omega-3 fatty acids in oily fish—lowered blood pressure, cholesterol, fat levels, and risk of heart attack. It can help rheumatoid arthritis, colitis, and dermatitis, and alleviate depression, as well.

Preparation

In a large skillet, heat the oil and cook the onion and garlic over low heat for 5 minutes, stirring, until the onion softens, about five minutes.

Add the tomatoes, wine, water, and fish, and boil for about 10 minutes. If the mixture starts to dry out, add more water. The dish is ready when the fish is cooked through.

Mix in the parsley and lemon juice, add salt and pepper to taste.

Serving Suggestion

Serve fish stew with Rosy Rice. Eating fish often is a good habit to adopt.

Ingredients

1 tablespoon olive oil

1 small onion, finely chopped

1 large garlic clove, finely chopped

1 pound fresh tomatoes, peeled and roughly chopped, or good-quality canned tomatoes

½ cup dry white wine

1 cup water

1½ pounds fish (Get a selection of any type of prepackaged fillets at the supermarket, but make sure at least half are an oily, firm, full-flavored fish such as swordfish, salmon, or whitefish.)

half a bunch fresh parsley, chopped

juice of one lemon

salt and pepper

Edamame (Soy Bean Pods)

If your bad habit is a nervous one like biting your nails, get something better to do with your hands, such as opening soy bean pods.

Soy is such a health-giving food—it has saponins, which may block cholesterol absorption. It also contains high levels of phytosterols and protease inhibitors, which protect against cancer. Genistein, found in soy, is a phyto (plant) estrogen with the ability to balance the excess of estrogen that causes PMS.

If the thought of tofu makes you wince, this is a way to get all the health benefits of soy without wondering how to cook those white slabs. You can find edamame at Asian markets. Find a packet in the frozen foods case. Throw as many as you want in boiling, salted water, and cook for 5 minutes. They taste like fava beans and are addictive in the way pistachio nuts are: you find yourself unshelling yet another.

Serving Suggestion

Serve edamame to guests with wine at a party instead of the usual nuts and chips. Get everyone started on a new good habit.

Conquer your bad habits, or they'll eventually conquer you.

Conclusion

Life is all about contrast: light and dark, feast and famine, rosy moods and the blues. The extremes are what make the journey interesting. The exhilerating parts help you get through the lousy parts, and the low parts inspire appreciation for the times when everything's going well. A hot shower never feels so good as after you've been caught in a downpour. Watching the sun rise is a wondrous experience only if it's something you're not compelled to do daily. And going out on the town seven nights a week can become as stale as staying home every night.

Happiness isn't so much about the big things—landing the fabulous job or getting married—it's the way you ride out the highs and lows on a daily basis. Miserable people stay miserable, no matter what happens. Six months after winning the lottery, people with a chronic negative attitude are unhappy again.

The ability to ease yourself out of a bad mood is a mark of mental well-being, and I hope you've picked up some ideas on how to do that from this book. I urge you to develop your own recipes for raising your spirits, whether it's filling your mind with pleasant thoughts so there's no room for thoughts that make you feel inadequate, or filling your stomach with nutritious foods so there's no room for the non-nutritious.

You might decide to raise your spirits with a steady diet of simple pleasures. Maybe you will cook your way to contentment and share healthy meals with people you love.

You might decide to take responsibility for what you eat and for your own happiness. Or you can finally let go of worry and pay more attention to everything going on around you.

Whatever you decide, know that it's not always easy. I've found that one has to learn life's lessons, not just once but over and over. Some days you'll remember your new way of thinking, other days you'll slip back into old habits.

But, you can take solace in the thought that, *because* feelings and moods are rarely static, the ability to make yourself feel good again is always just around the corner.

Bibliography

You Can Feel Good Again by Richard Carlson, Ph.D. (Dutton/The Penguin Group 1993)

Better Homes and Gardens Food for Health & Healing (Meredith Books, 1999)

The Healing Foods Cookbook by the editors of Prevention Magazine (Rodale Press, 1991)

The American Medical Association Family Cookbook by Melanie Barnard and Brooke Dojny (Pocket Books, 1997)

Mood & Food: The Complete Guide to Eating Well and Feeling Your Best by Elizabeth Somer, M.A., R.D. (Owl Books/Henry Holt and Company, 1995)

Mood Foods by Dr. William Vayda (Ulysses Press, 1995)

About the Author

Jane Eldershaw is a writer, graphic designer, and artist who lives in Manhattan. She has worked on magazines and newspapers for many years, including *New Woman* magazine, which specializes in articles providing psychological and emotional support for women.

Visit her website at www.eldershaw.com.